Health Foods and Herbs

Health Foods and Herbs

KATHLEEN HUNTER

AN
ARC
BOOK
ARCO PUBLISHING COMPANY, INC.
219 Park Avenue South, New York, N.Y. 10003

An ARC Book
Published by Arco Publishing Company, Inc.
219 Park Avenue South, New York, N.Y. 10003

Eighth Printing, 1976

Library of Congress Catalog Card Number 63-15194
ISBN 0-668-01083-5

Printed in the United States of America

Contents

FOR T.T.M.
WITH GRATITUDE

INTRODUCTION

I have long felt the need of an informative book on rational living, and I was very glad to be asked to write one myself.

I would say at the outset that, although some of the health treatments and diets suggested here are not entirely orthodox, I am writing from practical experience over a period of many years.

Having endeavoured to write in plain language shorn of all technical details that assume specialised training, I venture to hope that my phrasing will be understood by everyone. I have deliberately refrained from all highly technical formulae, and I have in all cases been entirely factual. If I give any opinions, these are based upon my comprehension of the facts which I have found in my researches among the writings of the highest authorities in the world.

I will grant that the theme of this small book is vegetarian and herbal, the reason being that over a long term of years I have established that there is no better course of diet for me and for a large number of my friends. The herbal remedies which I advocate have been tried and found excellent and efficacious. They may be slow-acting, but they are sure—and safe. Mother Nature is always the best judge of what will keep us in health, and no man-made drugs will ever equal her chemical factory.

ACKNOWLEDGMENTS

I am indebted to Mr. J. I. Rodale, one of the greatest nutritionists and advocates of healthy living in America for permission to quote from his most excellent and monumental work, *The Health Finder*. I have also been much helped by my friend Mrs. Bridget Amies, a great authority on fruitarian and vegetarian cookery. Her little books on *Fruit and Vegetable Juices* and 63 *Meatless Meals* are the best value I know. My thanks are due to Messrs. Fowler whose Treacle, Golden Syrup and Molasses products are so well known, for permission to include some of their excellent recipes.

My friend Mrs. Doris Grant, whose forthright books on diet, such as *Your Daily Bread, Dear Housewives* and *Housewives Beware* are so well worth reading, has very kindly allowed me to draw on these for some of my facts, and to give extracts from some of her works. Messrs. Mapletons Nut Food Co., Ltd., have also been most helpful, and their special recipes in the chapter on nuts and honey are very good indeed. Mr. Gilbert Harris, the owner of the Khormaksor herd of goats, which supplies the milk for his famous yogurt, has given me great assistance in the compilation of the chapter on yogurt.

The chapter on homeopathy will be found interesting, I think. I am indebted for much of the information to Mr. Foster, N.D., D.O., the Senior Consultant to the Homeopathic Clinique in London. The A. A. Supply Co., Ltd., have furnished me with much information regarding caffeine-free coffee (H.A.G.) which product allows me to drink coffee freely without doing any damage to my health. For the chapter on "Poison in the Kitchen," Dr. Gilbert's Health Foods, Ltd., manufacturers of a non-toxic salt, provided information.

Finally I have to acknowledge my great indebtedness to Mr. J. J. O'Dowd of Tralee, Eire, for supplying some excellent recipes for carragean. Mr. O'Dowd is one of the leading sea foods and seaweed merchants in the Republic of Ireland, and I doubt whether such a collection of first-class health recipes dealing with seaweed has been published before.

I think that I have acknowledged all sources of information, but if I have missed any they are errors of omission, not commission, for which I apologize in advance.

KATHLEEN HUNTER

CHAPTER 1

Health Foods, Herbs and Modern Foods

A time there was ere England's Griefs began
When every rood of ground maintained its man.
For him, light labour spread her wholesome store,
Just gave what life required, and gave no more.
His best companions innocence and health
And his best riches, ignorance of wealth.

Oliver Goldsmith wrote these lines some 200 years ago,
and this was about the time when the industrial revolution
was starting in Britain.

At the beginning of the 18th century, food was plentiful
and cheap and wholesome, although it must be said that
there had been other times when this was not so. For
hundreds of years previously the people of these islands
had been living year in and year out on the danger line of
under-nourishment and the troubles which it brought,
including deficiency diseases like scurvy.

In those earlier days the poor man in the towns rarely
had either fresh vegetables or fruit. The countryman had
his little plot of onions and leeks, but it was the Dutch
gardeners who brought garden vegetables to Britain in the
17th century. At the opening of the 18th century the
growing of garden vegetables had spread greatly. They
were being produced in the small plots of the villagers, and
many market gardens were springing up, and garden produce was appearing in the towns at a reasonable price.

The labouring classes both in towns and country ate
well. There were large supplies of cheap dairy produce
and vegetables, including quantities of potatoes, and of
course in the North the guid Scots oatmeal. The North-

erner drank more milk, but had less meat than the Southerner. Even so, the working man with his healthy foods had more nutriment in his diet, in the shape of calcium, iron and vitamins, than is estimated to be necessary in this age of scientific research.

And the health of the people was as good as the health of the long-lived peasant peoples of Europe at the present day. Look at the physique of some of the inhabitants of South-Eastern Europe. They don't get much meat—they can't afford it, and they have no factories taking the goodness out of the grain to sell it back to them at an enhanced price as vitamin B and wheat germ. Their staple diet is a coarse whole grain bread, thick vegetable stews and soups, goat's milk cheese and y o g u r t also made from goat's milk and therefore tuberculin free. Their lands " just give what life requires," but they are strong and hardy.

These people never buy fertilizers—again, they can't afford them—with the result that their ground imparts nourishment to the crops it grows, and incidentally they are not plagued with diseases of the soil that they have in Britain, those diseases which need such expensive preparations to cope with them, which in turn start other troubles that need still more expensive preparations ad infinitum.

Paracelsus began the chemical idea in the sixteenth century, but it was a long time after he died (at 51) before his notions began to be seriously investigated. With the coming of the industrial revolution the trouble started.

It became the ambition of the countryman to be able to afford red meat and fine white wheaten bread, and as a result the stone mills that ground slowly and exceeding small gave place to the steel rollers that flattened the germ into a disc instead of reducing it to powder, and even in those days they had adulterants. Among other additives, such as ground bone meal, the bakers used vast quantities of alum to produce a beautiful " pure " white loaf! All the same, it must be emphasised that even then the flour, which was mainly stone ground, was far better than much of what we are offered at the present day.

Modern large-scale food production methods have made it almost impossible to obtain a really pure and un-adulterated product of Nature. Everything is now made so easy and timesaving—it is so much easier to open a tin than to shell a pound of fresh garden peas or slice French beans freshly picked.

It is much easier also to buy a bag of powdered chem-icals and scatter the contents over the field, and it has almost immediate results on the crops and on the land. I had a very severe example of this when I removed from my country cottage in Cornwall, where I had worked land that had been composted for generations, to Argyll, and acquired a large garden that had been laced with chemical fertilisers for many years. The ground was absolutely dead, and it cost me a large sum of money to bring it into good heart again after several years, with the help of farmyard manure, seaweed and compost which we made from the weeds.

Chemicals act like a tonic, and give plants a sharp uplift, but the effect soon wears off and the soil is left as impoverished as before. Probably even more important, ground without any organic treatment is devoid of earth-worms, which are essential to the health of the soil. Pick up a spadeful of well-rotted farmyard manure, and several fat worms will be found. These spend their lives in making organic manure. They are the greatest gardeners of all; they eat soil to a vast extent and make about their own weight in the finest fertiliser every day, their castings being much richer than the actual soil they take in. Anyone doubting this can easily obtain proof by sending a worm cast from his garden to the local Agricultural Officer for analysis and a report. Charles Darwin established by intensive research that worms will pass through their bodies some 15 tons of dry earth per acre every year, and I think you will agree, therefore, that anything tending to encourage this unpaid fertiliser and aerator of the soil is well worth while. Compost, seaweed and farmyard manure are the breeding grounds for earthworms but chemical *kill* them.

In one of the greenhouses I acquired, which had been used for tomato growing and well laced with chemical manure, there was not a single earthworm when we came to dig the ground, and the soil was so poor that even the weeds were few. We took the old soil out and dug in about 6 tons of the finest rotted horse manure to a depth of some 2 ft. before replacing fresh soil, which was laced with a seaweed soil conditioner. There are now thousands of worms actively producing fertiliser and aerating the earth.

Apart altogether from the much greater nutritive value of foods grown by natural methods, there is a vast improvement in the flavour. Whenever possible, therefore, either grow or buy organically produced vegetables. Bread should, ideally, be made at home from 100% wholemeal flour. It is not easy to procure flour made from organically grown wheat, and the demand exceeds the supply, but it is possible to get 100% wholemeal unadulterated flour, and a loaf of this baked at home—and it is surprisingly easy to make—far surpasses in flavour and nutrition the " pure " white loaf of commerce, because ordinary white flour has had practically everything of value removed during the milling. This residue is subsequently sold separately at a high price and called vitamin B, a most necessary item of diet which will be explained when we are discussing vitamins.

This would be bad enough in itself, but what is added to the flour is much worse. As fast as one chemical is

prohibited by law (generally several years after its poisonous effect has been fully demonstrated) another one is put
forward. Look at what happened with agene—for five
years after it had been conclusively proved that the stuff
was a rank poison, its use was allowed and when it was
finally stamped on, another bleaching ingredient, chlorine
dioxide, was introduced, and is in use at the present time
(1962).

Many have been the campaigns over the past sixty years
against adulteration of flour to make a " beautiful white
loaf." Just prior to the Great War of 1914, Lord North-
cliffe ran a series of articles on what came to be known as
" Standard " bread containing wheat germ and semolina.
It had a dirty white look about it but it was on the right
lines; at any rate, nothing was added to the flour. A white
loaf, the whiter the better, is associated with purity, and
nothing could be farther from the truth.

In my household all the bread is made at home by our-
selves, and we know just exactly what we are eating. I
have been to the millers and seen a sack of wheat arrive,
be taken up to the top of the mill and gradually come down
through rollers of varying fineness until its arrival at ground
level where it is packed into 3-lb. bags, untouched by hand
at any stage. Making bread is very easy—it takes me about
a quarter of an hour every few days—and everyone who
comes to my house exclaims at the wonderful bread. My
friend Doris Grant in one of her most excellent books,
Your Daily Bread, gives her recipe for the " Grant Loaf,"
and there is nothing to compare with it: 100% whole
wheat flour, $\frac{1}{2}$ oz. dried yeast, 2 pints of water to 3 lbs.
flour, and salt to taste. It's as simple as that, and it's a
real food.

There are several 100% whole wheat flours available in
the U. S., all excellent. Such flour retains all the wheat
germ and the consequent vitamins B and E. It is a live

15

substance; bleached white flour is dead.

That great food scientist, the late Sir Edward Mellanby, proved that nitrogen trichloride (agene) induced fits in dogs. The bakers retorted that dogs were not persons. Quite correct, but I have no use for a product that gives fits to anything.

This is not all. We have dealt only with the flour and what the millers do with it. It passes to the bakers, devitaminised and beautifully bleached to " pure " white. The dough must now be conditioned by the use of chemical " improvers." These tend to make the bread retain its freshness over a longer period. My own experience has been that white bread which I bought to try out did not grow stale so much as it grew whiskers after a very short time in the bread bin. I can't experiment with my own wholemeal bread at home because it never lasts long enough.

Another thing that is allowed to be added is powdered chalk, i.e. calcium. This is regarded with great suspicion by heart specialists, one of whom wrote in a book on the subject that they have established beyond doubt that calcium raises the blood pressure. Nearly fifty million people in Great Britain, quite a number of them suffering from high blood pressure, have got to eat what will gravely injure their health and shorten their lives. It's a slow poison, ingested in homeopathic doses every day. Some people, of course, do have an actual calcium deficiency which can be remedied by a course of an organic product such as bone meal, not by an inorganic substance like chalk.

Calcium may be all right for growing children, but for older people who don't require it surely it seems hard to have no freedom of choice, unless they bake their own bread.

Nor is it sufficient to buy "brown" bread. This can be

doctored too, and often is. There are wholewheat breads which are called wholewheat but do not have all the wheat germ. Insist on well-known reliable flours, and always make sure you know what is in your bread. Remember the old Scot saying: *The whiter the bread, the sooner you're dead. . . .*

CHAPTER 2

Vitamins

To have an adequate grasp of the principles of health foods it is necessary to comprehend fully the use and action of the vitamins. That great biochemist, the late Sir Robert MacCarrison, said in one of his lectures: " I have used every occasion to emphasise that it is the lesser degrees of vitamin deficiency, and the less obvious manifestation of such deficiency that are of importance in western countries. A recognition of this fact is, I believe, essential to the prevention and cure of many commoner sicknesses of mankind—sicknesses to which we cannot always attach a diagnostic label."

Fifty years ago vitamins were unknown. Up to the close of last century people ate fruits, vegetables and cereals in the raw and unadulterated form with all the goodness retained. Canned foodstuffs were not as general by any means as they are now, and we have a lot of diseases at the present day that were not prevalent 60 years ago. About the beginning of the 20th century scientists began to suspect that there might be more in foodstuffs than minerals, fats, proteins and carbohydrates, and they started a series of experiments with animals that led immediately to a line of investigation that has had far-reaching results.

People nowadays talk familiarly about vitamins, but my great-grandfather, who had never heard the word, carried on eating his wholesome vegetables from his garden and making his bread from wholewheat flour, and lived to a ripe old age without being troubled by any of the diseases which are now so common. When, therefore, the scientists found that animals fed on processed foods containing sufficient proteins, carbohydrates, minerals, etc. died in the laboratory, it became certain that there was something besides these elements, and that, whatever it was, it was vital. This may consist only of " trace " elements, but unless there is the minutest amount of boron and cobalt and other trace items in the soil there will be no crops, and the animal organisation cannot live.

Eventually, it was found that vitamins are organic food substances, which is, of course, to say that they exist only in living things. They exist in foods in minute quantities but they are absolutely necessary for life. In the old days of long sea journeys men suffered severely from scurvy and died of it. As recently as the World War of 1914 nearly 8,000 soldiers perished from scurvy, although it was known by then that lemon juice was a remedy. Captain Cook, on one of his voyages, had the right idea, although he did not know the reason. He took with him a supply of barley grains, allowed them to sprout and made a brew of the sprouts, which he fed to his crew. They had no more scurvy. Scientists working on lemon juice isolated something in a crystalline substance which they tried out on guinea pigs, and found that this immunised them from scurvy. And so vitamin C (ascorbic acid) was discovered. It is interesting to note that guinea pigs were used, as these, human beings and apes, are the only animals that do not make their own vitamin C in their bodies, and must therefore get it in their food.

Plants manufacture their own supplies of vitamins. Some are richer than others in various types and these are now well-known. Hence the importance of a supply of fresh vegetables and fruits in the diet. Vitamins, unlike the fats, proteins and carbohydrates, are not foods as such— they are not broken down into other substances. They keep their own form and bring about certain essential changes in

19

the cells. Many of the functions and attributes of the vitamins discovered to date are now well-known and will be described in dealing with the individual types. Vitamins are manufactured by plants and here I would mention most strongly that there is no comparison between vitamins produced synthetically in the laboratory and those made by Mother Nature in her plant factory. Most of the known vitamins are now made synthetically and can be bought in any chemist's shop, but it is far better to have them naturally in the appropriate foods, and far, far cheaper also.

There is another point I would like to make. Vitamins are not food, and although food lacking in vitamins is useless so are vitamins by themselves. One cannot live on vitamins alone. And in the case of some types, D for example, one can have an excess which is as harmful as a deficiency.

"Refined" foods have generally had every vitamin refined out of them. White flour, white sugar and a lot of the breakfast cereals are very deficient in vitamins. For example, refined white sugar is the product that remains when all the B vitamins, and a lot of other valuable necessary trace elements as well, have been removed from the molasses. Food containing white sugar has, therefore, to be digested without the assistance of the vital B vitamins. The system must get these from somewhere and, as they are stored in the body in various places such as the liver and kidneys, these organs have to contribute the requirement, and hence a vitamin B deficiency occurs. The procedure is the same with all denatured foods, such as white flour.

So much for vitamins in general, now to examine them in particular.

Vitamin A. This vitamin can be obtained from both

animal and plant sources. In plants it comes from carotene.

Broadly speaking, it can be stated that about 5,000 I.U.'s (International Units) are the daily requirement for a man or woman; pregnant and nursing women about half as much more. It is found in carrots, spinach, turnip tops (far more than the actual roots), dandelions, melons (especially watermelons), parsley, tomatoes, lettuce; in fact, any kind of greens and to a lesser degree almost any kind of raw fruit. This is one of the easiest vitamins to obtain and, although as with almost everything else it is best when contained in a raw food diet, vitamin A is not lost to any great extent when food is cooked.

At the beginning of this century children were regularly dosed with cod liver oil, and a horrible dose it was at that. Parents were insistent that it " did them good," though I am sure they did not know why. If someone had told them that the children would have got just as much benefit from a balanced diet of, for example, carrots, kale, parsley, liver and endive, with a raw fruit salad to follow and preceded by a glass of tomato juice, they would have been very surprised. But such is the fact. A sufficient supply of vitamin A is essential for growth and particularly for teeth.

The Vitamin B Group. This is a most important vitamin and a deficiency of it gives rise to many distressing complaints—constant lassitude, weak heart, lack of milk in nursing mothers, nervous disorders, constipation, hair falling out, insomnia, eye troubles, even cataract, and a general lack of vitality and stamina.

As the amounts of B vitamins contained in foods are not great, it is frequently necessary to supplement the diet with added supplies. The best and richest sources are brewer's yeast, desiccated liver, wheat germ and offal such as liver and heart. It is to be emphasised that, unlike vitamins A and D, and like C, vitamin B is partly destroyed in the body, passes out in the excreta, and must be renewed daily. Where there is a shortage all kinds of distressing disorders happen, indigestion, colitis, a tendency to dropsy and heart trouble among them. A certain amount of B vitamin is stored in the liver and other organs and, as I mentioned earlier, this store is raided every time white sugar and other foods from which the vitamin B has been removed are eaten.

In the early days of the vitamin search, there was only one B vitamin, but further detailed research now shows that there are many varieties of this—B_1 to B_{12}—and there are divisions of these.

B_1 is known as aneurin, B_2 as riboflavin. By many careful experiments in scientific laboratories, it has been conclusively proved that the vitamin B group is absolutely necessary for health and it imparts to the system the power to combat and withstand disease.

Editor J. I. Rodale in his monumental work *The Health Finder* quotes an astounding case of the efficacy of vitamin B and vitamin C as reported in the *Medical Record* for 19th November, 1941. A young man whose spine had been fractured in an accident was a patient in a general hospital in Toronto, Canada. The accident had resulted in complete paralysis and loss of all sensation in the lower part of his body, including the muscles that control the functions of urination and excretion. Lying in bed for almost a year he had contracted bedsores. He had 14 of them, some deep enough to expose the muscle to a depth of some two inches. The sores were inflamed and filled with pus. He was emaciated and feverish, with a weak and rapid pulse. He had no appetite. Dr. W. J. McCormick, who wrote the article, had studied the effects of vitamin B_1 and vitamin C in curing open skin sores, so he directed that the patient be given these two vitamins in addition to a diet that stressed wheat germ, brewer's yeast, fresh fruits, green vegetables, milk and egg yolks. Within one week there was an amazing change for the better in the bed sores. The discharge gradually became less, the diseased tissue disappeared and healthy new tissue began to fill the ugly craters.

In about three months the largest sores had decreased to half their original size and one had closed entirely. In addition, the improvement in the patient's general condition was almost incredible. There was great improvement in the condition of his urine, and temperature and pulse rate became normal. Within a week from the beginning of the vitamin therapy he was able to move his toes for the first time in six months and gradually he recovered the use of other muscles. It is believed that the patient may have been suffering from a lack of vitamins B and C when he met with the accident.

Again, the drugs and sedatives he was given had greatly increased the demand of his body for these vitamins. Dr. McCormick says that it has been conclusively shown that even moderate doses of barbiturates and narcotics may increase the bodily requirements of vitamin B_1 by as much as 40%. Everyone who smokes or drinks increases the body's demand for vitamin B. Everyone who takes sleeping pills containing barbiturates must suffer from a considerable vitamin B deficiency which will naturally make such a person more nervous, and he will have to take more sleeping pills, which will decrease his supply even more in a vicious circle. The remedy is perfectly simple. Just eat foods that are rich in the B vitamins. Don't take synthetic vitamins. Eat the natural sources— brewer's yeast and desiccated liver. It is as simple as that. A large section of the people suffers from vitamin B deficiency owing to the refining and devitalising of many of the foods offered these days, and the loss must be made good by the daily intake of wholewheat bread (preferably from stone ground flour), beans, greens, most of the fruits, tomatoes and concentrates like brewer's yeast and desiccated liver. One thing that is no use at all is polished rice, as far as vitamins are concerned. There is the classic case of the prisoners sentenced to death in the Philippines in 1912 who were offered instead the opportunity of becoming diet guinea pigs. They were fed on refined and denatured foods, mainly polished rice. In six weeks all of them had signs of anaemia, dropsy, muscular weakness and finally their hearts grew feeble. When they had reached the point of collapse they were given just natural brown rice and they all rapidly recovered perfect health.

Again, there is the account of the epidemic of poliomyelitis—infantile paralysis—in the island of Nauru in the Pacific, between the Solomon and Gilbert Islands, under Australian administration, in 1910, when polio was hardly known. In two weeks 700 of the 1,500 on the island were struck down, and 38 died. The victims were all natives, with one or two exceptions. A few Europeans were affected, but not a single Chinese. The examination of the food of the natives showed that it was seriously lacking in the B group of vitamins, while the Europeans had a much more varied diet. The Chinese, being the market gardeners of the island, ate large quantities of their own vegetables, grown in strictly composted soil. The natives at one time drank large quantities of the local beer that was well laced with yeast, but they drank so much that it was forbidden by the Government. The Government now took action, and the sale of white flour and polished rice was prohibited. The improvement in the health of the people was immediate. Infant mortality fell from 50% to 7%, leprosy and tuberculosis, which had been rife, disappeared, and so did polio.

I would emphasise that these are not fairy tales. They are official reports of actual occurrences noted by qualified medical men with no bias and no axe to grind. Many thousands of pounds are spent annually now on polio vaccines. I suggest that if all denatured and refined foods were absolutely prohibited by law with the sternest penalties, and all bleachers, chemicals and improvers were forbidden to be used in flours, the vaccines could stay on the shelves of the laboratories, and we would all sleep the sounder for it.

Going back to Dr. W. J. McCormick again—in 1938 he had a young boy brought to him for treatment, suffering from polio in an acute stage. He was in a bad way with fever, headaches, vomiting, sore throat, stiff neck and pains in his arms and legs. After only five days of vitamin B_1 therapy, muscle pains, which had been so severe that he had to have codeine, eased and then disappeared, and in less than three weeks he was discharged cured and completely free from any signs of polio. This is a medical fact on official record in the hospital in Toronto.

I want to emphasise most strongly that all through this book I shall endeavour to present facts only, substantiated by really reliable authorities, whose case histories are on record for the information of anyone sufficiently interested.

We know a great deal about the action of vitamins since their discovery some sixty years ago, and the value of their use in orthodox medicine is now becoming widespread. Most excellent and painstaking research at the highest level has resulted in dramatic discoveries.

An article written by Dr. Alice Fay Morgan in the American magazine *Science* gives an account of an experiment in which the diets of certain animals were carefully controlled to include or exclude members of the B complex of vitamins. First, it should be made clear that an organic diet contains all the B complex vitamins, while a synthetically produced vitamin may not. These, then, were the results—three animals received the full diet along with adequate amounts of all the vitamins and they all were alive and well at the end of the experiment. Two animals had the full diet except for niacin, pantothenic acid and the filtrate factor. (Niacin and pantothenic acid are two of the B vitamins. The filtrate factor is that part of the B complex which has not yet been thoroughly investigated). These two animals were alive and well, but developed grey hair, became inactive, with elderly, sedate behaviour and impaired digestion. Four animals received ample diet in every respect except pantothenic acid and the filtrate factor. Three of these died from paralysis. The fourth, when near death from paralysis, was given the filtrate factor and a year later was alive and well. Moreover, her greying hair had turned black again. Four of the animals were given all the vitamins except niacin. Two of them died from paralysis, the third was showing similar signs and the fourth, which was given pantothenic acid rather than the filtrate factor, was alive and well. The last two animals received pantothenic acid and niacin but no filtrate factor. After six months on this diet both animals showed signs of progressive paralysis and hair that was not grey but dull and powdery instead of glistening black.

Another experiment was reported in the *Journal of Experimental Chemistry* for August, 1952. Rats which were normal and rats which were deficient in pantothenic acid were fed varying amounts of cholesterol. The normally fed rats developed fatty livers as a result of a very high cholesterol diet, but the rats which were deficient in pantothenic acid did not develop fatty livers. And when the pantothenic acid was removed from the normally fed rats the fatty livers returned to normal. The scientists concluded that these experiments showed simply that members of the

B vitamin complex should all be taken together or there is danger of serious upsets in nutrition and general health. Therefore take only food supplements made from natural foods—never synthetics.

It follows, arising out of this, that "enriched" foods should never be taken. In processing the cereals all the vitamins are removed from the grain, but not all are replaced synthetically, only a few. The foregoing experiments show that taking one of the B vitamins without the others can be positively dangerous. Incidentally, "enriched" foods are prohibited in Canada. Eat only whole-grain cereals and flours. Brewer's yeast and desiccated liver are the main and best sources of vitamin B and they include all the members of the complex.

In 1948 vitamin B$_{12}$ was isolated in liver. Out of many tons of liver a few tiny grains of a red crystalline substance were obtained. Dr. Randolph West, a celebrated authority on anaemia, who had been working in collaboration with the Merck Laboratories, injected five millionths of an ounce of this new substance into the muscle of a victim of pernicious anaemia and in six weeks' time the patient was restored to normal good health.

Many official experiments have been carried out on B$_{12}$ therapy. French doctors tried it with success for multiple sclerosis, polyneuritis and spino-cerebellar disorders. American scientists dosed a number of undernourished children in Ohio and they responded immediately. A professor in the University of Arkansas proved with laboratory animals that reproduction and lactation is entirely successful with a diet containing quantities of B$_{12}$ and folic acid, while control animals on the same diet but minus these two vitamins failed badly. The sum total of investigations and research so far indicates that all the B vitamins are absolutely essential for health, are closely related to one another, cannot operate separately and must be combined in the correct proportions in which they exist in natural foods.

Very often it is necessary to supplement food with added vitamins and it is perfectly easy to obtain all the requirements from natural food sources. Brewer's yeast is one great natural source, and for anaemia there is nothing to compare with liver; these two sources have all the B complex group vitamins. The cobalt, phosphorus and nitrogen chemical formula in B_{12} has not yet been determined and it has not been made synthetically. And it is so easy to obtain that there is no point in doing anything else. An adequate diet consists of plenty of fresh vegetables, wholewheat bread, brewer's yeast, liver extracts—or, of course, cooked liver and fish. A very good natural and appetising source is Marmite and also Yeastrel, both products of brewer's yeast.

Vitamin C. This is the wonderful substance which saved Captain Cook and his men from scurvy on their long voyages of discovery. They boiled the shoots of sprouted beans and ate the shoots and drank the water. Then it was found that lemon juice had the same effect.

In our own day we know that one of the greatest sources of vitamin C is the rose hip from the common *rosa rugosa*; there can be up to 6,000 milligrams of vitamin C in 100 grams of rose hips. Kale, again, is a fruitful source of supply, also brussels sprouts, raw cabbage and mustard greens especially. Sweet peppers are very good, as are dandelion greens and turnip tops (much better than the root). The minimum need for a man is about 80 milligrams per day, but this can be increased and do nothing but good. Unlike vitamin D, too much vitamin C will do no harm, especially if it is taken from natural sources. Unlike vitamin A and B, this vitamin perishes easily. It is water soluble, contact with copper kills it, and so does a pinch of baking soda in the cooking water. When cooking greens and cabbages, save the water and make it a base for soup.

Like the vitamin B complex, vitamin C is very potent against polio. It can be administered in massive doses. and vitamin C is sovereign against the common cold. Rose hip syrup can be obtained easily and cheaply these days from any chemist and there is no finer source of protection. This also contains vitamin A. Mark this— the ordinary common or garden rose hip is often low in vitamin C, but the wild rose, *rosa rugosa* especially, is extremely rich in both A and C. This syrup can be added to fruit soups, juices, jams and jellies.

Vitamin C is also necessary for the proper absorption of iron in the body and it is therefore very necessary in cases of anaemia, which may be caused by a lack of this vitamin even although there may be plenty of iron in the system.

Remember, however, that vitamin C has no keeping qualities. If you wash a lettuce in cold water most of the vitamin C has gone down the drain. Both copper and aluminium destroy vitamin C on contact. Use enamel (see that there are no chips in it) and glass. Now note this also: very little vitamin C is stored in the body (unlike A and B) and it is necessary to have a daily intake. This is all the more essential when it is understood that human beings, in company with guinea pigs and monkeys, do not manufacture their own vitamin C as do other animals and therefore they must have it daily in their foods.

Once again, the need is for ample quantities of fresh fruits and raw vegetables.

Vitamin D. This is sometimes called the Sunshine Vitamin. It is practically non-existent in plants. Cod liver or halibut liver oil is the most potent source, but even then in minute quantities. A tablespoonful of cod liver oil con-

tains less than a millionth of an ounce of the pure vitamin.
Excessive amounts of vitamin D are toxic.

The story of vitamin D and sunlight is most interesting.
Doctors found that exposure to sunlight cured rickets
but they did not know why, or why the dark-skinned were
more prone to rickets than those with fair skins. After
many careful experiments it was brought out that rickets
could be cured by: (1) sunlight, (2) cod liver oil, (3) ultra-
violet rays, (4) food irradiated by ultra-violet rays.
Finally it was proved that it was in sterols (waxy material
associated with fats in food) that the vitamin was present.

It was further discovered that the provitamin was present
in an impurity in cholesterol, and this was further isolated
and ergosterol was found to be the parent substance of
vitamin D. Ergosterol is derived from ergot, a fungus that
grows on rye. This was isolated and it was established that
the vitamin D_2 in fish oils is identical with the vitamin D
in ergosterol when irradiated by ultra-violet rays.

Almost every food we eat contains some quantity or even
just a trace of vitamin D which is stored in the body but
not used. Therefore you can get too much vitamin D
through too much sunlight, and many people do by
exposing themselves immoderately to sunlight on holidays.

There is not much known about this vitamin as yet,
compared with our extensive knowledge of the other types.
It prevents rickets, not, it is thought, by itself, but by
assisting the body to assimilate phosphorus, the mineral
which combines with calcium in the body. But, *ex nihilo
nihil fit*; it can't assist phosphorus to combine with anything if the phosphorus is not there in the first place. It is,
therefore, entirely necessary to have an adequate intake of
both phosphorus and calcium to enable the vitamin D to
function. And here is an interesting thing. Fur-bearing
animals get their vitamin D from the sun, but they
must lick their coats or the sunshine does no good.

Many animals hibernate during the winter months, when there is little benefit to be derived from the sun's rays. If they are given daily doses of vitamin D they will not hibernate because there will be no need for it.

With human beings the oil glands of the skin secrete the substance that becomes vitamin D in the presence of sunlight. Now mark this fact—if, after a long spell of sunbathing, which of course has resulted in the manufacture of a lot of vitamin D, a shower bath is taken with lots of soap, all the vitamin D disappears and the sunbath is wasted as far as that is concerned. In the tropics natives spend long days naked, or almost naked, in the sun and in the water, but they don't use soap and they never suffer from a lack of vitamin D. And don't forget, the more tan you acquire the less vitamin D is absorbed.

Vitamin E. This is the Fertility Vitamin—tocopherol is its chemical name, which is derived from three Greek words, and there are several types of tocopherols, to which letters of the Greek alphabet have been given— Alpha, Beta, Gamma and Delta.

Vitamin E has a distinct and definite effect on fertility during gestation. A silver fox breeder once told me that if they got their foxes fighting fit at the beginning of the mating season but omitted adequate vitamin E foods in the diet, the animals mated all right but when conception did occur, and the vixen had every evidence of being pregnant, there were no cubs resulting. The embryos perished and were reabsorbed into the system of the would-be mother. If the dog fox was starved of the vitamin there was no conception at all. If the embryo was not reabsorbed in the vixen a miscarriage occurred, and the result was the same —no cubs.

In human beings lack of vitamin E causes miscarriages and this can be remedied by eating foods that are well laced with the vitamin, such as wholewheat bread (white is useless and no source of vitamin E), raw green food and daily doses of wheat germ. Going back to the fox farm again, I was informed that they fed their animals on minced meat to which was added the contents of a sheep's stomach procured from the local slaughterhouse, together with the tripe, of course, giving massive doses of several vitamins. Litters of 8 cubs were successfully reared (the average number being 3 to 4).

In women, vitamin E is most effective in connection with menstruation and also with the menopause. A woman at the climacteric need have no fear of trouble if she has lived on a diet rich in vitamin A and E. This means ample supplies of raw salads and fruits and vegetables, and wholewheat bread, which last, of course, contains the potent wheat germ, the greatest source of vitamin E.

A few actual figures taken from official records will be interesting. In the countries where no white bread is eaten, in Russia for instance, in the 1930/40 decade the birth rates were about 30 per thousand of the population. During the same period the rate in London was 13 and in Paris only 11. The Russian peasant eats almost wholly " black " bread made from rye, with all the vitamin E complex and natural minerals. When they started making " pure white bread " in the 1870's the British birth rate was around 36 per thousand. At the beginning of the Second World War it was down to 14 per thousand. During the war the National bread of 85% extraction was made compulsory and almost immediately there was a big rise in the birth rate.

In the case of the peasants of France who live in the country and eat wholewheat bread and fresh green salads with every meal, miscarriages are almost unknown. The same applies to the Northern countries, Norway, Sweden and Denmark, and also to the Slavonic and Balkan districts. If then, you want to make sure of a large and healthy family this is what you need!

A lot more can be said about the uses of Vitamin E in connection with fertility, but the foregoing facts are all I have space for in this little book.

There is another and most important attribute of this vitamin and that is its great value for the treatment of coronary troubles. At the great Shute Clinic in Canada, where Dr. Shute and his brother, also an M.D., carry on their wonderful work of curing heart diseases, the uses of vitamin E are being more and more investigated and its potentialities are becoming understood to a much greater degree.

In this connection I cannot do better than quote from the *Vitamin E Bulletin*, the official organ of the Vitamin E Society of Canada, this address by Dr. Wilfrid E. Shute, Chief Cardiologist of the Shute Institute for Clinical and Laboratory Medicine at London, Ontario. Dr. Shute is a former wrestling champion who teamed up with his brother Evan Shute and with Arthur Vogelsang in developing the use of vitamin E extracted from wheat germ for heart disease cures. After describing coronary thrombosis, he calls the treatment of vitamin E "... the most important discovery in this century. ..." Thrombosis was first described in 1912. It did not appear at autopsy in 1900—yet in 1951 it killed half the males who died over the age of 40. The disease is increasing rapidly and is the greatest single cause of death in the world to-day.

Dr. Evan Shute, in his monumental work *Alpha Tocopherol in Cardiovascular Disease*, published in Canada by the Shute Foundation for Medical Research, London, Ontario, tells the wonderful story of their investigations into treatments for heart and vascular diseases with vitamin E. This book is written by a qualified medical

33

doctor for doctors as well as for laymen. I would advise everyone interested to obtain a copy.

The successes which the Shute brothers have had with agonising diseases like angina pectoris, thrombosis and high blood pressure are counted by the thousand, obtained by administering vitamin E in massive doses of nearly 100 milligrams after every meal for at least 30 days, thereafter reducing the dose gradually. When it is realised that the doses for many vitamins are measured in fractions of milligrams, the magnitude of the Shutes' dose will be appreciated. They have definitely proved that, in the great majority of cases which they have treated, vitamin E in very large doses is entirely successful in curing the diseases of the heart and arteries and blood, and if taken regularly in small daily doses, is a sovereign preventive. It is to be emphasised, however, that those who include in their daily diets quantities of fruit, green salads and ample whole wheat bread don't need to augment their intake of vitamin E further.

CHAPTER 3

Fats

These are most important, and unsaturated fatty acids are essential from a nutrition standpoint because the body cannot manufacture them. They occur in unprocessed natural fats, generally of vegetable origin such as cereal and vegetable oils like sunflower seed oil (than which there is no better source), olive and peanut oils.

These are the fatty substances which are powerful in preventing cholesterol deposits in the blood vessels. Animal fats contain little of these fatty acids and this is one reason why it is believed that a diet high in animal fats and low in vegetable fats causes cholesterol deposits. When vegetable fats are hydrogenated, i.e. made solid, they are changed chemically and the essential fatty acids are largely destroyed.

Cholesterol is a strange substance. It is absolutely necessary to life, but the formation of cholesterol deposits on the walls of the arteries can cause serious impairment of blood flow and actually cause heart disease in time. In one investigation made of persons who died of coronary thrombosis it was brought out that the cholesterol content in the coronary arteries was found to be no less than *four times* the average found in persons with normal heart function. Actually the body itself manufactures cholesterol to a degree far greater than one could consume in foods. A person on a high fat diet seldom gets more than 800 mg. per day of cholesterol from what he eats, while the normal liver is producing up to 3,000 mg. by itself. Now the body which is functioning normally puts all this cholesterol to good use. It is necessary for the manufacture of vitamin D, the sex and adrenal hormones and the bile salts.

Note that the cholesterol the body manufactures does not collect in the arteries, nor does the cholesterol which comes in natural foods. It is the cholesterol we receive from processed foods which is the cause of the trouble. And this is the reason why. Each time that the cholesterol occurs in the natural state in vegetable oils, etc. it is accompanied by lecithin, a substance which breaks cholesterol into small particles which move easily in the bloodstream and are readily absorbed in the tissues as and when required. When fats are hydrogenated, a common practice in today's processing, the lecithin is discarded. The cholesterol received in this way is dangerous. When it comes into the body by itself there is no provision made for using it and it floats aimlessly around the bloodstream collecting in clumps on the arterial wall. Then, sooner or later, the trouble begins. To sum up, therefore, cholesterol is essential to life but *only* when accompanied by lecithin.

If you eat regularly considerable quantities of animal fat—butter, milk and fatty meats—and little in the way of the vegetable fats—raw nuts, sunflower seed oil, eggs— you are probably short of lecithin. Generally speaking a natural diet should supply all the lecithin necessary.

CHAPTER 4

Fruitarian Diet

The advantages of a fruitarian diet are very many. Persons living chiefly on fruit and especially on raw fruit juices do not injure themselves by consuming the waste-products contained in and produced by flesh foods. In other words they avoid auto-intoxication. Digestion is very easy and hence the amount of work put on the digestive organs is much lessened.

Fruit juice helps to eliminate urates and to cleanse the blood of impurities. It is therefore of great use in cases of hardening of the arteries and rheumatics. It was noted in World War I that wounded Turkish soldiers healed very much more quickly than British, the reason being that they were nourished chiefly on fruits such as dates, figs, etc. as against the heavy meat diet of the English.

It is not too much to affirm that a change to a strict fruitarian diet will go far to cure diseases such as chronic tonsilitis, colitis, appendicitis, high (and low) blood pressure, anaemia, asthma, bronchitis, catarrh, obesity, constipation, hemorrhoids and coronary affections. This is an impressive list, but it does not by any means exhaust the potentialities of a rational meat-free regime.

Later on in this book I will give a number of easy recipes which can be tried out; but I would stress that an occasional fruit or vegetable meal, although it cannot do any harm, cannot be expected to afford any relief from any symptoms. To achieve full benefit and success a course of several weeks is necessary—and incidentally I will guarantee that anyone who does try out the diet over a period will not return to conventional meals again.

Mistakes can, however, be made by those beginning a reformed diet: eating stewed acid fruits and cooked vegetables at the same meal for instance. An excess of porridge, beans or fried dishes can have bad effects. It is important to bear in mind that the daily food must contain enough of various necessary elements. Protein is one of these, and good sources of this are wholewheat bread, cheese, oatmeal, beans and peas, and especially lentils. There are various excellent nut foods offered by firms specialising in these, and I give a list at the end of this book. Various recipes are given by the manufacturers.

In a fruitarian-vegetarian diet I would sound a note of warning: don't eat too much. These foods are much more concentrated than flesh. Take, for example, the different food values of meat compared with cereals, nuts and vegetables. Lean meat is composed of over 70% water and its total nutriment value is under 30%. Nuts vary around the 6-7% mark for water and have as high as 91% nutritive value in the case of Brazils. Wholemeal bread has about half the water content of lean meat and double the nutritive value. Obviously, therefore, in view of the high nutriment value of cereals a much smaller amount is necessary, and the consuming of excessive quantities of starch in the form of porridge and potatoes, or of such concentrated foods as haricots, nuts and lentils is liable to bring on a severe attack of dyspepsia. I think that a few suggestions for those who contemplate starting a meatless diet will be helpful and welcome.

For the reasons given above eat less. The same amount of nourishment will be obtained with half the cereal foods. For those employed in offices I recommend that at midday fruit should be taken, either raw fresh fruit or dried raisins, figs, dates, prunes, etc. and a few nuts at the same time. This will be ample until the evening meal, which can be enjoyed at leisure and can consist of a savoury nut rissole with vegetables, preceded by a glassful of raw carrot juice or a bowl of raw potassium broth, which consists of 7 oz. carrot juice, 4 oz. celery juice, 2 oz. parsley and 3 oz. spinach juice.

Remember that a meatless diet does not mean simply eliminating all flesh foods. You have got to have sufficient proteins in the daily meals. There is very little protein in fruits and vegetables. Figs and dates have the most of this category, but the main protein in a meatless meal will come from the beans, lentils and nuts.

Oatmeal is also well up the list, eggs have about the same protein content, and cheese has the highest of all. (But not " processed " cheese.)

I have regularly every day a bowl of vegetable soup made by simmering beans or lentils and any vegetable in season, and herbs, flavoured with a yeast or vegetable extract such as Marmite or Yeastrel, in a casserole.

At least twice a week the evening meal should consist of a raw salad composed of any of the green vegetables in season, with herbs and nuts. This will supply all the necessary vitamins and proteins (in the nuts). Two ounces of protein are required each day. The nuts can be ground up in a nut mill and flaked over the salad, and grated Parmesan cheese can be used in the same way. It is interesting to note that this cheese is the richest of all, containing nearly 50% protein.

Remember—be moderate. It is possible to have too much of both protein and carbohydrate. Excess protein causes nervous prostration and drowsiness after meals, often constipation and headaches. Too much carbohydrate i.e., starch, will cause dyspepsia, flatulence, pain in the chest, acidity and an inflammatory state of the whole system. Too little carbohydrate will cause lack of vital force and physical exhaustion. And above all be sure that an ample supply of wholewheat bread is taken every day.

I cannot be too emphatic about this. Proteins are muscle builders, and produce strength. Carbohydrates (and fats) produce heat and energy.

Phosphates and Mineral Salts. These are contained in wholewheat bread, cheese and apples. The essential salts are also contained in vegetables, so don't throw out the cabbage water or anything else in which vegetables have been cooked. It will make excellent stock for soups. I cannot be too emphatic about this. The amount of nourishing mineral matter which daily goes down the drain is most regrettable. Throwing out the baby with the bath water!

CHAPTER 5

Fruit and Vegetable Juices

The best way to start the day is with a glassful of raw fruit juice. We use an electric juicer to prepare our juices, but many of them are obtainable at health food stores. Apple and carrot mixed, plus some celery to avoid rheumatism, will provide a large proportion of the daily requirements of vitamins and a lot of minerals.

Celery, for instance, contains vitamins A, B, B_2 and C and no less than 12 of the mineral salts, including potassium, magnesium, sodium and chlorine. There is a faint trace of iodine, but the best source of this is a seaweed tablet. Carrot juice also contains many minerals. In addition to potassium, magnesium and chlorine it has phosphorus and calcium, and is therefore very suitable for combining with a vitamin D treatment.

Carrot Juice. The vitamin content of carrot juice is very extensive. It has A, B, C, D, E, G and K in abundance, and the amount of vitamin A is as much as can be assimilated by the body at any one time. Carrot juice is a very strong cleansing food and a very fine nerve tonic. It is excellent in the treatment of ulcerous conditions, anaemia, stones and circulatory troubles and the calcium content makes good bone structure in babies and also restores the calcium drain on nursing mothers. It is an excellent corrective of acidity and, as it contains a sort of insulin compound, is useful in the treatment of diabetes.

It is important to use the tops of the carrots for juice, as well as the roots, and this applies to practically every raw

41

vegetable. I cannot too strongly advocate the regular use of carrot juice. It is excellent for very many troubles of almost every organ of the body. It is practically impossible to take an overdose—even six or seven pints a day will do only good. And when carrot juice is combined with other raw vegetables such as apples, celery, beetroot, turnip (tops) and fresh lettuce, and taken over a long period regularly, there will be created a feeling of energy and well-being that has to be experienced to be believed.

While the above is the standard mixture, there are also various other combinations with carrots for definite diseases. A few are given here:

Anaemia: carrot and beetroot juice.

Rheumatism and kidney trouble: carrot and parsley.

Slimming and constipation: carrot and spinach, with lettuce for insomnia.

Blood cleansing and skin clearing: carrots and cucumber (also diuretic).

Arthritis: carrot and celery.

One of the most powerful combinations is carrot and dandelion—just the ordinary dandelion of the field. This is very effective.

Dandelion Juice has a very high content of potassium, sodium, iron and vitamin A. It is very rich in magnesium which, in combination with the minerals in carrots, makes it most valuable in cases of bone disease. The humble dandelion is one of the greatest sources of curative medicines available and it's easily the cheapest. Just go out into the fields and pick the weed. Every part of it can be used, if you can drink a coffee substitute, which I cannot, although it is much better, containing no caffeine or other heart stimulant. In passing I would mention that, as it is possible to obtain a caffeine-free coffee, there is no reason to be without this comfort of civilization.

Dandelion juice contains a high proportion of iron, sodium, potassium and vitamin A. It is therefore excellent in treating anaemia, helping poor blood conditions and circulation troubles. It is an excellent liver tonic, and useful for kidney and bladder troubles. Combined with carrot and spinach juice it is a very strong tonic, in the proportions of 1 oz. dandelion juice to 3 oz. each of carrot and spinach.

Lettuce Juice. This is exceptionally high in vitamin A, more so than many other greens. It also contains vitamins B, B$_2$ and C, and nearly all the mineral salts. It is very high in iron and magnesium. It is most useful and efficacious in the treatment of anaemia, obesity, goitre, dropsy and urinary disorders. Taken with carrot and dandelion juice in large quantities, up to 4 pints a day, it will be of the greatest benefit in cases of tuberculosis. It is sovereign in the treatment of rheumatism and arthritis.

Watercress. Another most excellent juice, with vitamin A very high. It has a large number of the necessary minerals, sulphur predominating, with high iron content. Chlorine, potassium, calcium and phosphorus are also present, with about 8% sodium and 5% magnesium. Being a strong alkaline owing to its high potassium content it is useful for acidity and purifying the blood. Used with carrot and spinach it is very good for low blood pressure and anaemia.

Parsley. This is by far the richest vegetable source of vitamin A; it is also a potent source of iron, sodium and sulphur. Note, however, that parsley juice is so strong that it should never be consumed in any large quantity by itself. It is a very powerful nerve stimulant and therefore is worse than strong coffee at night, and should not be taken just before retiring. Being rich in chlorophyll it is a good treatment for hardening of the arteries, and consequently for high blood pressure. It is a specific for migraine and a cure for many troubles connected with the eyes. It must be understood that it cannot be taken straight. It is much too potent. One part parsley juice, say 1 tablespoonful, with six parts each of carrot and celery juice is about right, and up to one pint daily of this mixture should be the amount consumed as a curative.

Spinach Juice. Except the herb Good King Henry (*Chenopodium Bonus Henricus*) there is nothing with a higher iron content than spinach in the garden. It has an enormous vitamin A content—2 oz. will afford enough vitamin A for one whole day. Spinach is the finest vegetable product known for internal cleansing. It is rich in minerals such as iron, calcium, sodium and iodine, and being such an excellent cleanser it is particularly curative in cases of duodenal ulcers, constipation, boils and abscesses, obesity—it is very good for slimming—and it adjusts blood pressure whether high or low. Taken with equal parts of carrot juice up to 2 pints daily over a period it will have most excellent results. As well as being exceptionally rich in vitamin A it is a source of vitamin B_2 and also contains vitamin K.

When it is realised that 1 lb. of fresh spinach contains upwards of 90,000 International Units of vitamin A and nearly 6,000 of vitamin C, its value will begin to be understood. Apart from Chinese mustard, which contains even more vitamin A and vitamin C, its nearest rival is turnip (tops) with just under 50,000 I.U.'s of vitamin A; but this is also much higher in vitamin C, running to nearly 14,000 units per lb.

Turnip Tops. In addition to having a very high content of both vitamins A and C, they are very rich in calcium, potassium, iodine and iron. Consequently they are excellent for the treatment of anaemia, liver and kidney troubles and goitre, although for this last complaint there is nothing to compare with seaweed, of which more later.

Turnip roots contain vitamin C, but in nothing like the quantity of the turnip tops—which are so often thrown away. Turnip juice from the root can be taken with advantage mixed half and half with carrot juice—a pint a day.

Tomatoes. Tomato juice has a very high content of vitamin A, up to 7,000 I.U.'s, very little B_1 and under 1,000 of vitamin C. But it is very rich in mineral salts, potassium and iron. It is recommended for rheumatism and arthritis, and for liver complaints, and is valuable as a purifier of the blood. Being a natural alkaliser it is used with much benefit to counteract any acid condition of the blood. But note that it should not be taken at the same meal as any starch (potatoes, etc. or sugar included), as these will tend to neutralise its alkaline effect. Made with half tomato and half apple juice, a tomato cocktail is an excellent apéritif. A pint a day of tomato juice can do nothing but good in the majority of cases.

Beetroot Juice. Taken in conjunction with celery and carrot juice, beetroot juice, containing as it does quite an amount of the vitamins A, C, E, B and B_2, plus nearly all the minerals, is most excellent for the treatment of nervous disorders, arthritis, hard arteries, kidney troubles, jaundice, gout, constipation and anaemia. Note, however, that as it contains a considerable amount of sugar it should not be taken by diabetics. It is also high in potassium and consequently is most useful in cases of impure blood stream.

Women who suffer from migraines at the menstrual period will derive much benefit from a pint a day, preferably mixed with carrot and celery juices.

Cabbage Juice. This most powerful juice should always be taken in conjunction with another, preferably carrot. It is then first class for relieving constipation. It is quite one of the most useful of vegetable juices, containing as it does vitamins B, B_2, C and E, and a large number of the mineral salts including sulphur and chloride. It is thus a very fine cleanser of the system. Use it in combination with spinach and lettuce juice. It is very good for slimming but remember that it is not sufficient just to take a glassful of this or any juice daily without adjusting the diet to assist. No starch, pastries or sugars. Use honey in place of sweeteners (never saccharin).

Nettles. I have already referred to a weed of the garden, the dandelion, which is a wonderful medicine. And now I would draw attention to another free plant of the greatest value, that can be had for the picking. The ordinary stinging nettle of the fields is one of the finest spring cleaners known to herbalists—very alkaline and a solvent of uric acid and therefore an excellent remedy for rheumatic ailments.

It is very high in vitamin A content and a glassful of two thirds carrot and one third nettle juice will make an excellent cleansing tonic.

I am indebted to my friend Mrs. Bridget Amies, the well-known dietician, for permission to reproduce the passages from her most excellent little work on *Fruit and Vegetable Juices* which are included in the following section. I strongly recommend anyone interested in food reform and meatless meals to obtain this book; it is packed with sound knowledge.

JUICES FOR SPECIFIC DISEASES

To obtain any benefit from this treatment, at least one pint of the juices must be taken daily. Two pints are better, and up to 4 pints may be taken. Combine them with a raw fruit and vegetable diet: no starches, sugar or protein. Where several juices are recommended it is best to take two or three of them and continue for two weeks, and then change to two or three others from the list.

Here are some recommendations from the list of Mrs. Amies:

Acidity. Spinach, carrot, celery, beetroot, lettuce, grape, orange, tomato, pear and peach.

Acne Spots. Carrot, watercress, spinach, celery, grapefruit and onion.

Anaemia. Carrot, spinach, beet, celery, parsley, turnip leaf, lettuce, apple, cherry, raisin, black grape, prune, fig, watercress, grapefruit, strawberry and blackberry.

Apéritif (to increase appetite). Two parts tomato juice to 1 part of grapefruit and one tablespoonful of parsley juice. Sip 4 oz. before meals.

Arthritis. Celery, cucumber, watercress, carrot, spinach, tomato, grapefruit, orange, lemon and apple.

Asthma. The following juices will greatly diminish and relieve this very troublesome complaint. Some will cure it if maintained over six months combined with a suitable diet. The causes of asthma are complex and deep-rooted, and the cause must be found to effect the cure. Dandelion, carrot, beetroot and cucumber—all to be taken raw and cold. Omit all foods containing high concentrations of starch. No cold milk to be drunk.

Bilious Attack. Look to your diet for a permanent cure. Take juices of the following: celery, apple, tomato, carrot, parsley, dandelion.

Blood Cleanser. Celery, cabbage, dandelion, watercress, parsley, beetroot, tomato, carrot, turnip leaf, garlic, lemon and apple.

High Blood Pressure. Combined with a completely raw diet, sufficient mental and physical rest, these invariably cure: celery, parsley, raisin, cucumber, dandelion, grapefruit, lemon, orange and pear.

Low Blood Pressure. Beetroot and grapefruit, and the diet as for high blood pressure.

Boils and Abscesses. Carrot, spinach, cucumber and garlic.

Bronchitis. People subject to this complaint should have a very small intake of starch and mostly a raw vegetable and fruit diet. Take daily: carrot, dandelion, grape, orange, lemon and pineapple.

Catarrh. Garlic, carrot, lettuce, apricot, radish, lemon, orange, pineapple and strawberry.

Rejuvenation. The Greeks, who had much knowledge which has been lost to us in these days, ate daily one whole raw cabbage. Due to its mineral salt content, cabbage is nature's great rejuvenator. Take equal parts of celery and cabbage juice, add a tablespoonful of lemon, and drink 4 oz. of this mixture three times daily between meals.

Rheumatism. Celery, carrot and parsley or cucumber, watercress and tomato.

Sciatica. Celery and spinach or, best of all, just common stinging nettles.

Slimming. First cut out all starch and sugar. If you want a sweetener use pure honey. Take a cupful of cabbage juice morning and evening. Or 6 tablespoonfuls of spinach juice. Or 3 tablespoonfuls each of cabbage, spinach and lettuce juice.

Note that the following are incompatible juices which must not be taken together:
  Prune with cabbage or onion.
  Pear with tomato.
  The citrus fruits (oranges, lemons, grapefruit) cannot be taken with turnip, watercress, cabbage or sprout juices.
  Apricot and the juice of any green leaves will not mix.

And here is the recipe for a *Muesli*, a grand thing to start off the day for the children, recommended by that great Swiss dietician Dr. Bircher-Benner:

Muesli

2 or 3 apples. 1 tablespoonful of ground walnuts, hazel nuts, almonds, Brazil nuts, or mixed. 1 tablespoonful of good Scottish oatmeal (soaked before-hand for 12 hours in 3 tablespoonfuls of water. 1 tablespoonful milk. Juice of half a lemon.

This will be enough for 3 to 4 children and should be given night and morning. Clean the apples by rubbing them with a dry cloth, but see that they really are clean in view of the sprays which are used these days. Mix milk and lemon juice with oats, grate apples (with peel, core and pips), stir and serve immediately; sprinkle with the nuts last thing before serving.

RAW VEGETABLE AND FRUIT JUICE SOUPS

These soups are something out of the ordinary and very good for health. They are grand spring tonics and are useful for the treatment of catarrh and colds. Note that they are all prepared from raw ingredients and all the goodness which is often destroyed in cooking is preserved.

These soups are very nourishing and when used in the daily fare follow them with a light meal only. I give just one or two, but from these ideas will evolve others from which delicious soups can be made.

Vegetable Juice Soup

6 tablespoonfuls of carrot juice. 3 tablespoonfuls of turnip juice. 3 tablespoonfuls of cabbage juice. 4 tablespoonfuls of celery juice. 1 egg yolk. 1 gill milk.

Prepare the juices, beat the egg yolk up with the milk and blend slowly with the juices, beating all the time. Serve with finely chopped parsley.

Carrot Juice Soup

1 cup carrot juice. 1 cup milk. Nutmeg to taste.

Blend together and dress with chopped mint.

Cabbage Juice Soup

1 cup cabbage juice. 1 teaspoonful sunflower seed oil (or olive, but sunflower is best). 1 teaspoonful lemon juice. Yeastrel or Marmite to taste.

Blend together and serve with finely-grated cheese, Parmesan for choice.

Beetroot Juice Soup

1 cup beetroot juice. 1 tablespoonful chopped seedless raisins. 1 cup milk. 1 tablespoonful grated Parmesan cheese.

Blend all together and sieve. Enough for 2 persons. Excellent for anaemia.

Potassium Broth

1 cup carrot juice. 1 cup cabbage juice. 1 tablespoonful parsley juice. ½ cup spinach juice. 1 cup celery juice. Yeastrel or Marmite to taste. Add a little milk if desired.

This is a grand blood purifier, eliminator, and excellent for the kidneys. The celery is very high in mineral content and is a very fine nerve tonic.

Here are two mixed fruit and vegetable juices flavoured with aromatic herbs, that will be found most refreshing and rejuvenating:

FRUIT AND VEGETABLE JUICE

(1) 6 tablespoonfuls of tomato juice. ½ teaspoonful of lemon juice. 2 tablespoonfuls of sunflower seed oil (or olive, but sunflower is best). Chopped tarragon, rosemary and basil.

(2) 3 tablespoonfuls of beetroot juice (leaves and root). 3 tablespoonfuls of lettuce juice. 2 teaspoonfuls of onion juice. ½ cup milk. Finely chopped marjoram and mint to taste.

As a useful guide here are the amounts of juices obtained by the use of a modern centrifugal juice extractor— 3½ oz. of juice from each of the following:

          5½ oz. Tomatoes.
          7 oz. Lettuce.
          7 oz. Spinach.
         10 oz. Beetroot.
         14 oz. Carrots.
         14 oz. Onions.

CHAPTER 6

Black Molasses and White Sugar

Mr. J. I. Rodale wrote an informative booklet entitled: *Sugar : The Curse of Civilization*, and he did certainly make out a most impressive case against refined white sugar and sweetening generally. The following extracts are reproduced by permission:

" We call white sugar a ' drug ' because in the refining process everything of food value has been removed except the carbohydrates—pure calories, without vitamins, minerals, proteins, fats, enzymes or any of the other elements that make up food. Pure carbohydrates do not exist in nature, so it is our belief, and that of many nutrition experts, that white sugar is extremely harmful—as harmful as a drug, especially in the quantities in which it is consumed at the present day. Each cell in the human body is equipped to deal with *natural* foodstuffs. Certain vitamins and minerals are necessary for the body's use of fats, certain others for protein, certain others for carbohydrates.

Natural foods (fruits and vegetables, honey, sugar cane and maple syrup for instance) come ready equipped with all the things necessary for their metabolism—the calcium, the B vitamins, the enzymes, the phosphorus—and so forth. In the case of the sugar beet and the sugar cane, we have unhappily discovered how to remove all these parts of what started out as perfectly good food, and leave nothing but the sweet taste—and the calories. Our cells, accustomed over hundreds of thousands of

53

years to dealing with natural foods, cannot handle such a substance.

What happens is slow starvation of the cells, starving for all the natural good food value that should be present in foods. Can such starvation bring cancer? We have no direct proof that just eating white sugar by itself will cause cancer. But we know that animals kept on diets of refined foods such as white sugar have far more cancer than animals eating natural foods.

Obesity, diabetes, arthritis, tooth decay, pyorrhea, asthma—is it not possible that diseases like these are related to our enormous intake of white sugar?

Why not? Does it not seem probable that cells so deranged and sidetracked from their natural kind of nutrition will eventually become diseased? "

Editor Rodale then goes on to make the point that sugar is not necessary, as is often thought, for the creation of energy.

" For thousands of years before human beings knew how to refine sugar, man worked from sun to sun at jobs requiring infinitely more energy than present-day work requires. He never knew about white sugar. WHERE DID HE GET HIS ENERGY? "

Primitive man ate natural foods, fruits and vegetables which he grew and which were rich in minerals and other elements. Carrots, apples, grapes, figs, dates, plums, etc., these all have a sweet taste. In these days one cannot do better than follow the natural foods of Adam and Eve— leaving out the apple of discord they unfortunately consumed. We have now many more excellent varieties. I will guarantee that they had nothing better in Eden than a really ripe Cox's Orange Pippin!

Still in the Garden of Eden, it is highly probable that Adam knew about sweeteners of other types than vegetables and fruits. He very probably was acquainted with what the Indians now call " gur " or jaggery, with which they have been familiar for thousands of years. In many of the old writings reference can be found to jaggery. Apparently it matures like wine, is even sweeter than sugar and is completely unrefined. It has excellent nutritive qualities. The Indians use it for nursing mothers and it is fed in large quantities to stock. It is known to them as a blood purifier, is good for the treatment of rheumatism, and has a slightly laxative effect. It is simply the juice of palm trees boiled down to a concentrate. It is very high (over 75% in some varieties) in sucrose content. The Indians regard the sugar products as the " life giving energy of the sun."

Jaggery can be obtained in the U. S., and the time may come when it will be a regular article of commerce rivalling black molasses with which, of course, it has much in common.

Now, suppose you concentrate the sugar occurring naturally in fruits and vegetables, throwing away everything else. Of course you manufacture sucrose this way, or glucose. But you will have only a " pure " substance left—a drug, just as white sugar is. Therein lies the terrible danger from the use of white sugar—its unnatural concentration. Concentrated pure sugar is a drug unrelated to anything that occurs naturally. For this reason it makes terrible demands on your body.

First, it throws off the calcium-phosphorus balance and disrupts this entire important phase of your body machinery. Secondly, because refined sugar has been robbed of the B vitamins that are so necessary for its assimilation by the body, it latches on to these wherever it finds them, namely in your digestive tract, so that the person who eats refined sugar is bound to be short of the B vitamins. Result? Nervousness, skin troubles, digestive troubles and a host of other disorders which lead to much more serious trouble later on.

Given a full natural diet with plenty of fruit and vegetables, especially carrots, sugar of any kind is unnecessary. My friend John Tobe of Niagara, dietician, herbalist and world traveller, who visited me recently on his second trip round the world, told me that when he was in Hunza (that Happy Valley between the Karakorams and the Hindu Kush mountain ranges) he found the most healthy race of people that he had ever seen. Their food in general consisted of raw fruits (dried apricots in the winter) including mulberries, peaches, plums, pears and cherries. Cereals and vegetables were wheat, peas, broad beans, lucerne, buckwheat, millet, barley, rice, onions, potatoes, carrots, turnips and lettuce.

These people get their sugar requirements from the natural sweetness of the fruits and raw vegetables. Food is generally raw, simply because they have very little fuel of any kind. They are almost vegetarians because they can't afford to use meat, and on this diet they live a busy active life for upwards of 100 years. Diseases such as afflict our civilisation are practically unknown, and until some of their young men began to filter through the mountain passes to the outer world, and, returning, brought back some of the civilised diseases, they never needed a doctor. Strong and healthy as they were when they left Hunza, they fell victims to the various sicknesses which happened to be rife among the community in which they took up residence. This proves that it is the diet that matters and that given an entirely natural diet there is no need for the refined product of the sugar cane.

But I began this chapter with the raw unrefined product, molasses, which is a very different thing from the white erivative. Incidentally it is often referred to as crude molasses, which is unfit for human consumption until it has een cleaned (not processed—just cleaned) of all extranous matter which the Government calls "suspended olids," like bits of dead insects, metals which have loughed off tanks, etc. Straining would be a better decription of the method. Of course the finished product as just as much nutritive value as the raw unscreened or " crude " molasses, and its value is very high. Still, it is ot a cure-all as some have maintained, and in any case ou should not eat too much of it.

By the courtesy of Messrs. Fowler, whose West India reacle has held a Certificate of Purity, Quality and Merit f the Royal Institute of Public Health and Hygiene without a break for the past twenty-five years, I am able to give ere some of their most excellent recipes for this product, vhich I recommend as being healthful, easy to make, and nexpensive. A 20-page booklet containing these and many ther recipes for West India Golden Syrup and Treacle is vailable upon request from Messrs. Fowler, Ltd., Glassouse Wharf, Orchard Place, Blackwall, London, E.14.

Wholemeal Scones

6 oz. wholemeal flour. 1½ oz. butter or margarine. 1 level tablespoonful Fowler's West India Treacle. Approximately 3 oz. milk. ½ teaspoonful cream of tartar. ¼ teaspoonful bicarbonate of soda.

ieve cream of tartar and bicarbonate of soda into the our and mix well. Rub in fat. Make a well and add eacle and milk to make a soft dough. Shape on to a oured board, ½ inch thick, and cut into rounds. Bake on greased or floured tray in a hot oven (450°F.) for 10 to 15 ninutes.

Walnut Loaf

¾ lb. self-raising flour. ¼ lb. Fowler's West India Treacle.
2 oz. chopped walnuts. 2 eggs. 3 oz. Demerara sugar.
¼ pint milk. Pinch salt.

Mix together flour, salt and sugar. Make a well in the
centre and add the beaten eggs and the treacle. Mix
thoroughly with the milk and add the chopped nuts.
(Mixture should be of soft consistency.) Bake in a moderate oven for approximately 1¼ hours. For variation the
nuts may be omitted and any dried fruit added, or a few
chopped dates and chopped walnuts.

Family Fruit Cake

8 oz. self-raising flour. Pinch of salt. 4 oz. butter. 2 oz.
brown sugar. 6 oz. sultanas (or mixed fruit). 2 oz. candied peel. 3 tablespoonfuls Fowler's West India Treacle.
2 eggs, or 1 egg and milk instead of second egg.

Rub fat into flour, add salt, sugar, fruit and peel. Beat
egg or eggs and add to them the treacle, which has been
warmed slightly. Mix egg and treacle well together. Add
this mixture to the flour and fruit, stirring and beating to a
smooth consistency. Put into cake tin lined with buttered
paper. Bake 1½ to 2 hours in slow to moderate oven.

Gingerbread

½ lb. flour. 2 oz. margarine. 1 oz. Demerara sugar. 1 teaspoonful ground ginger. 1 teaspoonful bicarbonate of
soda. 2 tablespoonfuls boiling water. 1 oz. candied peel.
1 egg. 6 oz. Fowler's West India Treacle (¾ teacup).

Rub lard into flour, add dry ingredients, treacle (warmed) and beaten egg. Mix bicarbonate of soda in boiling water and add. Mix well together and bake for ¾ of an hour in a moderate oven.

Bitter Sweet Pudding

Into a fairly shallow oven-proof dish put a good layer of Fowler's Pure Cane Golden Syrup. Place on top of the syrup thickly-cut slices of bread, with the crusts trimmed off, spread over with butter or margarine on *both* sides. Beat up an egg and add a teacupful of milk. Pour this over the bread. Leave to stand for about ½ an hour, then bake in a moderate oven until the bread is crisp and golden brown on top. Serve hot with sections of lemon to squeeze on each portion of pudding.

Chocolate Mousse

1 dessertspoonful Fowler's West India Treacle. 2 oz. chocolate. 2 eggs.

Melt chocolate in bowl stood in hot water. Add 2 egg yolks, beat and stand the bowl in hot water for a few minutes. Whisk whites of eggs, add and beat well. Mix in treacle. Put into trifle cases, placing half a walnut on top of each, and leave to set.

Apple Chutney

6 lb. cooking apples. 2 lb. onions. 2 lb. brown sugar. 1 lb. Fowler's Pure Cane Golden Syrup. 1½ oz. ground ginger. ½ oz. ground cinnamon. ¼ teaspoonful cayenne pepper. 1½ oz. salt. 1 quart vinegar. ⅛ pint water.

Peel, core and slice the apples. Mince the onions. Cook
slowly together in the water. When apples and onions are
cooked down, add all the other ingredients and simmer
very gently, until mixture is well blended, soft and smooth.
Long slow cooking gives the best results. Bottle while hot
in clean warm jars.

Date and Treacle Chutney

1 lb. pitted dates. ¼ lb. raisins. ¼ lb. onions. ¼ lb.
sugar. ½ oz. garlic. ¼ oz. salt. 6 chillis. 1 pint vinegar.
2 tablespoonfuls Fowler's West India Treacle.

Dates, raisins, onions to be chopped finely. Boil with all
other ingredients until tender (on slow heat). Bottle in
clean, warm jars.

West India Chutney

12 bananas. 1 lb. dates. 1 lb. green cooking apples. 2 lb.
Spanish onions. ¼ lb. crystallised ginger chips. 1 teaspoonful curry powder. 2 tablespoonfuls salt. 1 pint
best vinegar. 1 lb. Fowler's West India Treacle.

Remove skins and cut bananas into half-inch strips, pit
and cut dates into small pieces. Peel and cut very thinly
the cooking apples and onions. Add ginger chips. Place in
a bowl, adding spice, salt, curry powder and treacle. Cover
all with vinegar mixed with about half a pint of water.
Stir all well together. Turn into a large jar or basin and
bake for about two hours in a slow oven until chutney is a
rich chocolate colour. Bottle and cover while hot.

Creamy Dessert Whip

1 egg white. Pinch of salt. 1 heaped dessertspoonful Fowler's Pure Cane Golden Syrup.

Place egg white and salt in a quart-size basin and beat with a rotary whisk until the mixture stands up in stiff points when the whisk is lifted up quickly. Bring syrup rapidly to the boil in a small saucepan, stirring continuously, then tip this quickly on to the egg white and continue beating until mixture is cool and white. This is delicious served with strawberries, bananas or any other fruit, either fresh or cooked, or in pies, etc. It is most economical as this quantity makes a large basin of lovely cream whip.

CHAPTER 7

Nuts and Honey

I remember one of my friends telling me about Joseph Thomson, the great Scottish explorer of Africa who was at school with my friend's father in the eighties of last century, relating his great astonishment that the natives in what is now called Tanganyika appeared to exist happily and healthily on cereals and vegetables and practically no meat at all. Every now and then on special feast days, or on ceremonial occasions, some unfortunate beast would be slaughtered and divided among the villagers, and on lucky days a hunter would return from the hills with a buck.

In those days, some 80 years ago, our knowledge of proteins and carbohydrates was somewhat scanty, and of course we knew nothing about vitamins until the early part of this century. The diet of the natives of Africa consisted then—and in the villages in the bush still does at the present day—of *mtama* (kaffir corn), maize, various native vegetables, sem-sem (sesame), a seed very rich in oil, nuts especially the ground or monkey nuts which they call *njugu* and the *mnazi* or coconut. Considerable quantities of ground nuts and coconuts have for long been exported to Europe mainly for their oil, but during the last 50 years they have been in increasing demand as the advantages of a vegetarian diet became more widely understood.

The native diet in Africa is of course supplemented by quantities of various fruits, such as the mango, pineapple, orange and lime. They have sugar cane which they suck raw and, of course, wild honey (*asali*). Beeswax is also an important article of commerce. In the War of 1914 when the Germans trailed all over East Africa, pursued by our forces, von Lettow Vorbeck, the resourceful German commander, kept his soldiers in trim by living off the cereals of the country for years. Meat was a scarce luxury and honey was a medical comfort. When a beehive was discovered (sometimes with the help of the asali bird) the honey was extracted, and sealed in hollow bamboos with beeswax.

Most nuts are very rich in proteins, carbohydrates, fats and a variety of the essential minerals in the correct proportions (like everything else in Nature). Honey contains only about one fifth water, the rest being composed of the various sugars (about 75%) and various mineral salts that have been identified, such as iodine, phosphates, iron, calcium and magnesium, together with an unknown proportion of unidentified but certainly very essential "traces."

The fruits are all high in natural sugar content, and on a diet of these products of the good earth native porters will travel hour after hour through the bush carrying 50-lb. loads on their heads, and still have enough energy at the close of day for an evening sing-song!

We have travelled a long way since Joseph Thomson's time, and our scientific researches into food analysis have solved many mysteries. But some vegetable products still have a residue which defies discovery; our chemists know that there is a something remaining in a " trace " quantity that is elusive but absolutely necessary, and only Nature can put it in the particular food. Chemists can not.

Take the " simple " honey for example. Chemical analysis can identify over 90% of its constituents, but there remains some 5% composed of substances about which we do not know anything. Honey is the imperishable substance. We know it's composition, to within 0·5% of plant acids, and the exact proportions of glucose (34%), fructose (40%), water, dextrin, sucrose and proteins. But however carefully you mix all these together in a laboratory, you

won't have honey. It may taste very similar, but it will not
have the nourishing or healing effect of Nature's product.

It is the same with vitamins and almost all the other
natural substances. There is always something that defies
detection, and it always will. Take that mysterious
substance which the bee manufactures, when required,
known as "Royal Jelly." The bees make this when
necessary to turn an ordinary larva—ordinary, mark well
for if left to develop without treatment it would come out
an ordinary worker bee with a working life of some six
weeks—into a superb queen bee with a working life of at
least three years, during which period she lays many
thousands of eggs, all precisely the same when they are
deposited in the cell. It is the elusive "something" which
transforms the embryo from a sexless little worker into a
highly fecund insect.

Don't have honey that has been what is termed "processed." It is cheaper to buy, bulk for bulk, but not for
nourishment. You cannot beat Nature. You can keep
honey in glass jars over the years, and it is excellent when
crystallised, but never heat it as this would kill the
(admittedly very small) amount of vitamin content. There
are, as far as we know at present, only about half a dozen
identified vitamins in honey, but they have an effect that
we don't understand fully either.

Honey is not a natural product which occurs in nature.
It is manufactured by one of the most wonderful of living
creatures, and the bee is not a honey-maker by instinct.
When the worker is born it is equipped with all the necessary impedimenta for honey-making, but it has to be
taught how to use them and it serves quite an apprentice-
ship before allowed away on its own to collect nectar.

Note that just any flower won't do; bees work on a
system, and when it is realised that it takes about a
thousand journeys from the hive to the flower bed to

collect one ounce of nectar that loses 50% in evaporation, it will be understood that a bee sweats for its living. No wonder that its working life in the summer is only a matter of weeks. Say the flower source is an average distance of $1\frac{1}{2}$ miles from the hive—that is anything over 3,000 miles for one ounce of nectar. That's work!

To those who can eat honey, and there are very few who cannot, it is nourishment of the most agreeable form. It is the quintessence of food. As a mild aperient it ranks as one of the best. Its sweetening properties as compared with any kind of sugar are by far superior in their action on the health. The reason is that all food, if not water soluble, requires to be changed within the body before its nutritive parts can be received into the system. This change is accomplished by the process of solution and is called, of course, digestion. Starch, which forms some three-quarters of white bread, is useless as food while it remains in the form of starch, undissolved. In the act of eating, saliva changes part of the starch into sugar, which in due course, being received in solution into the blood, supplies heat and power.

Honey in its natural state is already in the right condition for absorption into the system and requires no labour to render it into a heat-producing power. Hence the superiority of honey over all kinds of sugar food. But—and this is most important—the honey must be absolutely pure and not one of the compounds (usually containing glucose) sold as " processed " honey. Pure unadulterated honey, extracted from clean combs, or eaten in the form of sections, will produce a healthy condition of the body which no other food-stuff can do.

Apart from being a grand food, honey is also a curative agent for many things. If, when I am working with my bees I get stung, I immediately apply a generous blob of honey to the spot and forget about it. It is a splendid antiseptic.

The finest home-made wine I ever brewed was simply a mixture of apple juice and honey laced with some sherry yeast from the Grey Owl Laboratories. I am drinking it now after letting it mature for three years, and of course it is better than new. You will find the recipe in the chapter on Amateur Winemaking.

A friend who was a District Officer in East Africa once told me that practising Muslims are enjoined to praise their God before eating honey. (*Allah Akbar!*) And Mohammed himself gave honey and the bees special mention in the Koran, *vide* chapter XVI: " The Lord spake by inspiration unto the bee saying ' Provide thee houses in the mountains and in the trees and of these materials wherewith men build hives for thee, then eat of every kind of fruit and walk in the beaten paths of thy Lord.' There proceedeth from their bellies a liquor of various colours wherein is a medicine for men. The same being not only good food, but a useful remedy in several distempers particularly those occasioned by phlegm." There is a story that a man once came to Mohammed and told him that his brother was afflicted with a violent pain in his belly, upon which the prophet bade him give him some honey. The fellow took his advice, but soon after, coming again, told him that the medicine had done his brother no manner of service. " ' Go and give him more honey, for God speaks truth and thy brother's belly lies.' And the dose being repeated the man by God's mercy was immediately cured."

The Holy Bible tells us that John the Baptist lived on wild honey for some time. (Matt. iii, 4.) Children were fed on milk, cream and honey—" Butter and honey shall he eat that he may know to refuse the evil and choose the good." (Isaiah vii, 15.)

Of course it is well known that bee stings are reputed to cure rheumatism, a somewhat spartan form of treatment; the effect is probably due to the formic acid injected with the sting, and note that this formic acid is found by analysis in the honey itself—in homeopathic doses, admittedly. The acid content is only 0·5%, but it is there.

The soothing, easily-digested characteristic of honey makes it very useful in cases of stomach ulcers. It exercises a bland antiseptic action.

I have known a feverish cold stopped overnight by an infusion of peppermint well laced with honey. As we here take a lot of rose hips (vitamin C) we don't catch the common cold, but there would be no doubt about the remedy if we ever did.

For insomnia, try a glass of warm water in which some honey has been dissolved, plus a Passiflora tablet, made from the passion flower.

Honey is also very good for all forms of chest troubles, and the honey produced in the Scottish Highlands, where the hills are clothed with pine trees and heather, is the best of all. I recommend starting the day with a *muesli* of ground nuts, soaked oatmeal, lemon juice and honey—see page 49.

Returning to Joseph Thomson and his wonder that the natives could perform such feats of physical endurance, what he could not have known, in the then imperfect state of our chemical research, was that the nuts provided the proteins, carbohydrates and fats, and many of the essential minerals in a natural state. The ground nuts and coconuts of Africa comprise about half their weight in fats. Ground nuts are best in proteins, about 30%, and coconuts better in carbohydrates, also nearly 30%.

On page 69 will be found a table giving the values of various foods, comparing meats with nuts, by which it will be seen that the proteins of ground nuts at 28%, and the fats at 49%, are far in excess of beef at 30% and 8% respectively. Furthermore, it is to be emphasised that the fat content of nuts is vegetable fat, with the advantage over the animal fats of containing only unsaturated fatty acids, which means that deposits of cholesterol in the arteries are avoided, with the consequent elimination of the danger of coronary thrombosis on this score.

There are many varieties of edible nuts, but the best known and most used in Britain are almonds, chestnuts, Brazil nuts, walnuts, ground nuts, hazel nuts and coconuts. They all have their different qualities and contents. Brazil nuts, for instance, are somewhat low, compared with others, in proteins and carbohydrates, but they make up for it with their enormous fat content—about 61%, against the general run of 45-50%.

Brazil nuts contain about 6% carbohydrates as against chestnuts with about 75%. But the latter are lacking in fat, having only 7% against the 61% of Brazils. For this reason therefore, it is recommended that nuts should preferably be mixed before being grated or ground and added to the meal.

Naturally several varieties of oils are available from all these nuts, and all of them are preferable to those of animal origin, but the finest oil for salads and culinary work generally is without any doubt that expressed from the seeds of the sunflower. I use sunflower oil here to the exclusion of all other cooking and salad mediums. Olive oil makes me liverish, I find, and I have no such trouble with the sunflower.

The late Sir Jack Drummond, who was a former Scientific Adviser to the Ministry of Food, was quoted as saying: " It is of course impossible to challenge the statement that the human body can be adequately nourished on a purely vegetarian diet. Not only have we the obvious example of many vigorous native peoples who live wholly on plant food, but nutritional research has now established sound scientific foundation for believing that man can do without meat."

COMPARATIVE FOOD VALUES OF FLESH FOODS AND NUT KERNELS

(Table supplied by Mapletons, Ltd.)

	Water	Percentages of: Carbohydrate	Protein	Fat
Almonds	4·7	4·3	20·5	53·5
Peanuts	4·5	8·6	28·1	49·0
Brazils	8·5	4·1	13·8	61·5
Lemon Sole (Steamed)	—	—	19·9	0·9
Hake (Steamed)	—	—	18·5	3·3
Salmon (Tinned)	—	—	19·7	6·0
Beef Steak (Stewed)	—	—	30·8	8·6
Chicken (Roast)	—	—	29·6	7·3
Bread (White)	—	53·7	7·9	0·7
Bread (Wholemeal)	—	44·4	10·8	2·2

By the courtesy of Mapletons Nut Food Co. Ltd., I give here seven satisfying meals, being a week's menu made from Savormix, which can be obtained from any health food store. All these dishes have high protein value, and can be used with eggs, cheese, tomatoes, potatoes or any other vegetable. They are easily and quickly made.

SUNDAY

Nut Roast

1 lb. Savormix. Slightly less than ½ pint of cold milk or water. Sage and onion stuffing to taste. 1 dessertspoonful vegetable cooking fat. 1 dessertspoonful yeast extract.

Mix together all ingredients except vegetable cooking fat and yeast extract. Shape. Spread all over with vegetable cooking fat and yeast extract mixed together. Bake in hot oven for one hour or until well browned.

MONDAY

Nut Rolls

4 tablespoonfuls Savormix. 2 tablespoonfuls cold water.
1 tablespoonful Suenut (nut suet).

Roll pastry and cut into squares. Mix Savormix, water
and Suenut, put sufficient soaked Savormix on each square
of pastry and roll over. Bake in hot oven. Serve hot or
cold.

TUESDAY

Boiled Rolls

4 tablespoonfuls Savormix. 2 tablespoonfuls cold water.

Mix together and divide into 4 portions. Place each on a
square of greaseproof paper (4″ × 4″). Tie each end. Boil
for 10 minutes, serve hot or cold.

Fried Rolls

4 tablespoonfuls Savormix. 2 tablespoonfuls cold water.

Proceed as for previous recipe. When rolls are cold fry
them in vegetable fat until golden brown.

WEDNESDAY

Lentil and Savormix Roast
(*Sufficient for* 6 *to* 8 *people*)

¼ lb. red lentils. ¼ lb. Savormix. 1 large onion. ¼ pint
cold water. ¼ lb. tomatoes. Pepper and salt if desired.

70

Wash lentils and strain off water; place in casserole. Cut up onion and add to lentils, together with seasoning, and stir well. Place casserole in a warm oven where the temperature will gradually rise. Cook slowly until all the water has disappeared and the lentils are reduced to a pulp. Scald and skin tomatoes, reduce to a pulp and add to the lentils with 8 oz. Savormix. Beat well together with a fork. Grease a pie dish well and press the mixture well in. Place little knobs of vegetable cooking fat (Nutter) on top. Cover with greaseproof paper and bake for 1 hour in moderate oven. Serve with baked tomatoes and rich brown gravy (see recipe on page 72), or with steamed onions or parsnips and parsley sauce.

THURSDAY

Rissoles

4 teaspoonfuls Savormix. 2 tablespoonfuls cold water.

Mix well together and form into rissoles. Coat in bread crumb dressing. Fry in vegetable cooking fat.

FRIDAY

Nut Meat

8 tablespoonfuls Savormix. 4 tablespoonfuls cold water.

Mix together and fill into a stone jar or basin. Cover, or tie greaseproof paper over the top and boil for 3 hours. When cold it will turn out a perfect mould.

SATURDAY

Savormix Roast with Parsley and Lemon Forcemeat
(Sufficient for 6 to 8 people)

12 oz. Savormix. 1 full teacupful cold water.

Mix well and allow to stand while preparing stuffing.

Forcemeat
4 oz. bread crumbs. Season if desired with pepper and salt. 1 oz. Suenut (nut suet). 1 tablespoonful finely chopped parsley. A little grated nutmeg.

Mix all dry ingredients together, add beaten egg and a little milk if necessary to moisten.

Method for Roast. Grease pie dish. Cover bottom of dish with prepared Savormix; press down. Add prepared forcemeat, then the rest of the Savormix and press down well. Brush over top with a little milk. Cover with browned bread crumbs. Place little knobs of Nutter on top. Cover with greaseproof paper or an enamelled plate. Bake for one hour in moderate oven. Remove cover and brown for 10 minutes. Serve with rich brown gravy, for which the recipe follows. A little redcurrant jelly is a pleasant addition.

Rich Brown Gravy

One medium-sized onion. ¾ oz. plain flour. ¼ oz. butter. ¾ pint boiling water. 2 teaspoonfuls yeast extract.

Peel and cut up onion very finely. Place butter in small saucepan and make very hot. Add onion and brown well.

Add flour and brown slowly, so as not to burn. Dissolve yeast extract in hot water and add slowly to contents of saucepan. Bring to boil, stirring well. Boil for 10 minutes or longer, stirring occasionally, and adding more water if gravy is required thinner.

NOTE

These preparations, being made of nuts, are very much more concentrated and nourishing, bulk for bulk, than any meat meals. They will be found most satisfying and, except for a small amount of fat in the butter in the gravy, contain only unsaturated fatty acids. They should, of course, be accompanied by as many vegetables as possible.

When I am making these dishes for myself I always use tomato juice instead of water. I find it gives a much better flavour. If you don't like the tomato flavour keep to the plain water as recommended by Mapletons.

CHAPTER 8

Seaweed

It is difficult to refrain from using superlatives when writing about seaweed. There is nothing to compare with it for health. It is the greatest natural tonic and conditioner available to any living animal, and every animal knows it. See the cattle wandering over the flats at low tide to get the kelp on the sands. In the Orkneys there is a famous herd of sheep that cannot get past the dyke from the shore to the grass fields—they never want to either—and everyone knows the quality of Orkney and Shetland wools. My Dobermann bitch has a glossy black coat that shines like satin—that's seaweed!

Years ago, the " dulse man " was a familiar figure in the Scottish villages, and at the present time the Irish of the West Coast, the Gaedhealtacht fishing folk, gather the carrageen moss from the sea for blanc-mange, soups and a syrup for coughs and colds among many other culinary uses.

Just near my house here, on the shores of Loch Creran, there is a most modern factory for seaweed pharmaceutical preparations. For many years I have sold a grade of dried seaweed for manure and a liquefied solution for plant fertilisation, and there is now a wonderful seaweed preparation which conditions the poorest clay or sandy soil into a fine workable tilth.

Seaweed is very rich in chlorine and potassium, and of course it is a source of iodine and calcium. It has many other minerals including magnesium, phosphorus, iron, copper, sodium—naturally from the salt in the sea—and sulphur. In addition there are about a dozen of the

74

"trace" elements such as barium, boron, chromium, lithium, silicon, silver, strontium, etc. and remember that all these most necessary elements are organically produced —they have never seen a laboratory.

It is good to know that the value of kelp is being appreciated more and more each year, and new factories for the drying and crushing of the raw weed are being built in many parts of the world. The minerals that kelp contains have been demonstrated to be essential to human nutrition.

There are a large number of different seaweeds around the coast of Britain. I recently acquired 4 volumes exactly 100 years old, being the complete range of British Seaweeds, "nature printed" and I was surprised at the variety of types. It has been estimated that seaweeds were among the first living plants to appear on this earth and according to the record of the rocks they have altered very little since the beginning of time.

Information as to the actual make-up of seaweed will, I am sure, be welcome. It contains the starches and sugars (carbohydrates), but this sugar is not dangerous to diabetics since it does not increase the sugar content of the blood. It contains fats and proteins also in small quantities, and it has at least one of the unsaturated fatty acids. There are also indications of some vitamins, especially vitamin C.

These are all very necessary items in diet, but it is when we come to the minerals that we really see the value of kelp. Living and growing as it does in the sea (and even now our scientists have not finally established the content of sea water) the weed has absorbed all the minerals the water contains, digested them and made them capable of assimilation by all forms of animal life.

What follows sounds incredible, but it is true. If you burn carrots you get about 1% remaining as minerals, beetroot about the same and apples about half as much. Now, the residue after seaweed has been burnt is from 10% to 50% of mineral deposits. No wonder that where seaweed is available cows calve more easily, and give more milk, sheep have fleeces like silk, and little Willie, having had seaweed powdered on his porridge or been given some seaweed tablets, or a carrageen broth, has a more shining face than ever and creeps no more, unwillingly, to school.

Expert dieticians believe that a lack of trace elements and minerals in our daily food gives rise to many of the deadly diseases of today such as anaemia, thyroid disorder, of course, which causes goitre owing to a lack of iodine, and general coronary afflictions.

A little daily dose of a few tablets of pure seaweed will adjust all these conditions. It is just as simple as that. When a cold is threatened, or a troublesome cough (other than a smoker's cough, of course) try this:

Soak and rinse ¼ cup of carrageen seaweed moss, and add to 6 cups of water with the thinly pared rind and juice of 1 or 2 lemons. Boil for 10 minutes and allow to simmer for a further 10 minutes with honey added to taste. Then strain, and add 2 tablespoonfuls of garlic syrup which, like the carrageen, can be obtained at any chemists, and it will be found after taking this that not only does the cold disappear, but the whole system is toned up.

CARRAGEEN RECIPES

Egg and Carrageen Mold

1 pint water or milk. ½ oz. carrageen. 2 eggs. Sugar to taste. Sherry, rum or other flavoring.

Make as for Carrageen Milk Mold (page 79). Beat eggs after separating yolks from whites. Strain carrageen, etc.

on to beaten yolks, stirring well. Fold in stiffly-beaten whites and put into mold, adding flavoring as desired. Allow to set, then turn on to glass dish.

A more substantial sweet may be made by using half the quantity of milk.

Prawn and Carrageen Savoury

1 pint milk. ½ oz. carrageen. Anchovy essence. Bay leaf. Blade (i.e., sliced) mace. Carmine. Pepper and salt. Prawns.

Steep carrageen for 10 minutes and pick. Boil in milk flavoured with mace till soft and thick. Strain, and add anchovy essence and a few drops of carmine. Mould in small individual moulds. Turn out when set, lay a prawn on top of each and decorate with parsley.

Apricot Mold

¼ lb. apricots. 1½ pints water. ¾ oz. carrageen. Pinch baking soda. 2 oz. sugar. Almond essence.

Steep apricots overnight in 1½ pints water. Strain off liquid and cut apricots in small pieces. Stew fruit in steeping liquid till soft. Add carrageen, baking soda, sugar and almond essence. Boil till thick. Sieve, reheat and mold. Turn on to a high glass dish and decorate with whipped cream. (Tinned apricots may also be used in this recipe, or tinned pears or pineapple, in which case fruit need not be stewed but only chopped and boiled with the carrageen.)

Beet and Carrageen Mold

2 beetroot. 1½ pints water. 1 oz. carrageen. 3 tablespoonfuls vinegar. 1 bay leaf. Blade (i.e., sliced) mace. Pepper and salt. To garnish: lettuce and cress.

Steep carrageen for 10 minutes. Pick. Add to water to which flavourings have been added, and boil thick. Strain. Add vinegar to the cut up beetroot. Stir till liquid is coloured. Mold, and when set turn out and garnish with lettuce and cress.

Lobster Mold

1 pint milk. ½ oz. carrageen. Meat of 1 lobster. ⅓ pint cream. Carmine. Pepper and salt. Anchovy essence. Lettuce and cress.

Shred lobster meat finely, keeping back some meat pieces and claws to decorate mold. Boil carrageen in milk till thick. Strain, add pepper, salt and anchovy essence, shredded lobster, cream and carmine. Pour into prepared mold. When set, turn out and decorate with lettuce and cress. Stand lobster head in center of dish.

Carrageen Jelly

2 lemons. 1 orange. 1 oz. carrageen. 1 pint water. 6 oz. sugar. Green or orange colouring. Whipped cream.

Peel the orange and lemon rind very finely and put into a saucepan with the carrageen and the water. Bring to the boil, and boil for 25 minutes. Strain the juice of the lemons and orange on to the sugar and strain it into the boiling liquid.

Add a few drops of colouring. Pour into a fancy mould and leave in a cold place to set. Turn out when set and decorate with whipped cream.

Carrageen Milk Mold

1 pint milk. ¼ oz. carrageen. Lemon rind. Sugar to taste. Sherry or other flavoring. Coloring.

Steep the carrageen as in previous recipes. Put into a saucepan with the milk, and the lemon rind peeled very thinly, and boil until soft and thick. Strain and add the sherry and coloring.

Pour into a wet mold and leave in a cool place till set, then turn out and decorate as desired. When the soft fruit comes into season you can serve this mold with some steamed gooseberries, blackcurrants, etc.

Carrageen Milk Mold with Rhubarb

1 lb. rhubarb. ½ pint water. 1 oz. carrageen moss. 6 oz. sugar. Some pink coloring. Cloves to flavor.

This is a good sweet to make while the rhubarb is still tender. Stew the rhubarb, till soft, in water to which cloves have been added. Boil the carrageen with this until thick. Strain. Add the sugar and a little pink colouring. Reheat and then pour into a wet mold and leave in a cold place to set.

Turn out when set and decorate with roses of whipped cream or in any way you fancy.

Carrageen Drink

½ oz. carrageen. Juice of 1 lemon. 1 quart water. 1 oz. sugar. Juice and rind of 1 orange.

This is the best spring tonic you can take. Steep the carrageen as directed. Drain and pick it over. Put the carrageen, orange rind, sugar and water into a saucepan. Bring it to the boil and then simmer for 15 minutes. Strain and add the lemon and orange juice and serve hot or cold.

CHAPTER 9

Coffee

According to a statement in *The Oriental Herald*, quoted by *The Journal of Science* in 1829, coffee appears to have been first used in Venice about 1615 and in Paris in 1644, finally getting to London in 1652.

It is estimated that some twelve million pounds were imported annually into Europe before the plantations were established on a commercial scale in the colonies. The Dutch introduced it into Batavia about the year 1696, the French into Martinique in 1727 after it had been in the Île de Bourbon in 1717, and finally the English began planting in Jamaica in 1730. After which it was quickly introduced into Ceylon, Sumatra and Surinam. The plant is found native at San Domingo and in Abyssinia, Mozambique and Zanzibar.

Nowadays, of course, the chief sources of coffee are Brazil, Costa Rica, the West Indies generally, the old Dutch colonies in the East Indies, and Arabia, and it has turned the natives of the Wachagga tribe on the slopes of Kilimanjaro into very rich men, their coffee being of a very high quality.

Of recent years there has been much research into the benefits and the dangers of coffee drinking. It was known that drinking coffee late at night tended to prevent sound sleep, and it was finally established that the enemy in this connection was the drug caffeine, which among other things is a very strong heart stimulant. In fact it is used by the medical profession in cases of heart trouble. It dilates the coronary arteries and furnishes a better blood supply to the heart, but undiluted caffeine must only be taken under proper medical advice

Coffee drinking administers the daily homeopathic dose of caffeine and, the effect being cumulative, all sorts of troubles begin to happen in the long run. Coffee should be avoided by those who have heart disease, angina pectoris, high blood pressure, skin infections, arthritis and liver trouble.

It has been established that the caffeine in coffee causes an increase of up to 10% in the basic metabolic rate of the body within the first hour after coffee is taken. Another drawback to coffee is that it prevents iron being utilized in the body.

There was an article in the foremost medical journal in Britain some years ago in which a qualified medical practitioner wrote that it was difficult to understand how people who take coffee (or tea) with every meal can ever absorb iron from their food at all. This could lead to anaemia, a very unpleasant complication for a heart case.

The vitamin intake is also threatened. The coffee bean contains up to 2% caffeine, and it may well be that caffeine creates an inositol deficiency. (Inositol is one of the vitamins in the B group complex.) The experiments which suggested this showed that when coffee was added to the diet of dogs they developed a paralysis that was cured by inositol and an eye trouble that was cured by biotin (another B group vitamin), thus tending to establish that the inclusion of caffeine created a biotin and inositol deficiency.

Another trouble that has not been definitely proved scientifically, but which is strongly suspected, is that coffee prevents the utilization of calcium in the body, and this is very important. Lack of calcium can give rise to all sorts of bone troubles, and a deficiency is very dangerous to a heart case.

On the other hand, to many people, myself included, coffee is a very pleasant drink. It is therefore consoling to know that as a result of considerable scientific research a method of production has been evolved which eliminates the greater part of the caffeine content in the bean without in any way detracting from its aroma and bouquet. The variety of coffee known as NONKAF has been on the U.S. market for many years now and is excellent. Granted that perhaps it does not give the immediate "uplift" to the system that a cup of ordinary coffee will provide, but there is no point in drinking a harmful medicinal heart stimulant as a beverage.

A few facts more about coffee may be interesting. For instance, one kilogram of coffee contains an average of 12 grams of caffeine. Caffeine is a stimulant not a nutrient. As a stimulant, it primarily affects the nerves, but also the heart and other organs.

Caffeine robs many people of sleep and lessens the capacity for deep slumber, thus reducing the benefits to be gained by healthy sleep. Caffeine has no effect on the taste and aroma of coffee. Whether caffeine, either in the form of coffee, or as a medicine, is beneficial can only be decided by a qualified person in each individual case. Under proper medical care for instance, caffeine can be helpful in rectifying disorders of the circulation, but everything depends on the exact dose. Some 50 years ago, one Ludwig Roselius realising the harm that caffeine can do, invented a decaffeinated coffee which gently stimulates, without exciting. This process has, through the years, been continuously improved, and is now sold under the brand name of NONKAF, which can be purchased from Vim & Vigor Health Food Shop, 175 W. 57th St., New York, New York.

I would emphasise that the decaffeinating process involves no chemicals and the process is interesting. The raw unroasted coffee berries are first soaked by water or steam. This process opens the cells of the beans which then appear (under a magnifying glass) as channels through the berries. Next a harmless and very volatile caffeine solvent is driven through these channels and with it goes the caffeine content of the berries, which are then again steamed to remove any of the solvent which might otherwise remain. The beans are then dried and roasted in the usual manner and the coffee has lost none of its flavour.

CHAPTER 10

Cheese

Cheese, as everyone knows, is the dried curd of milk. This curd (casein) which is held in solution in the whey under natural conditions, or so long as the milk is fresh, coagulates by the addition of any acid. Lactic acid formed in the milk serves to precipitate the curd in the ordinary process of souring.

Curd appears as a first stage of digestion by the action of the gastric acid of the stomach. In cheese-making, rennet is used, a preparation from the stomach of the calf, but in Holland and other countries a weak solution of hydrochloric acid is used instead of rennet as a starter. No book on health foods would be complete without a discussion on cheese, but in a small work like this full justice to the subject cannot be done and a few general facts and observations will have to suffice.

Being one of the main milk products, cheese is of a very great antiquity. It is of course mentioned frequently in the Holy Bible. The athletes of olden times in the East trained on it for strength, and they were not weaklings by any means.

Being *kosher* it is of course an article of diet with the Jews. Having a considerable ratio of nourishment to bulk is also much used by expeditions. There are very many varieties available at the present day, and each has its own flavour and content. It is made from cow's milk, goat's milk (in Norway and Switzerland especially), and from sheep's milk in France, India and the East. The goat's milk cheese has a sort of chocolate color and a distinctive flavor which I, personally, like very much. It can be purchased in the U. S.

An analysis of a typical American cheese (Cheddar for example) might be given as follows: protein 27%, fat 36%, carbohydrates 4%, minerals, calcium and phosphorous, vitamins A, B and D.

This is a very nutritious food and an excellent substitute for meat. Owing to the high fat content it is not so easily digested.

Cream Cheese is high in fats and low in proteins and carbohydrates.

Italian Parmesan has about 35% each of proteins and fats and up to 140 calories per ounce. (Vit. A.)

Dutch Cheese has about 27% protein and 20% fats, with 10% salts and up to 40% water. (Vit. A.)

Stilton Cheese contains some 25% proteins, 45% fats and a small percentage of carbohydrates and salt. I do not think that any cheese in the world can compare with a really well matured Stilton. It is costly, but well worth every penny. Its flavour is much milder than, say, Limburger, and has a piquancy all its own It is often helped in maturity by a drink of good port wine.

All cheese is rich in calcium and phosphorus, and its calorific value is impressive when compared with that of animal flesh. Compare lean beef at 600 calories and 23 grams fat with Stilton cheese which contains up to 2,500 calories and 194 grams fat, both per lb. weight. And incidentally compare both with the Brazil nut with its 3,500 calories and 319 grams fat.

The following recipes for cheese will, I think, be of interest:

Savoury Cheese Rissoles

Put ½ pint of hot water and 2 oz. butter in a saucepan and bring to the boil. Sift in slowly 5 oz. of flour and cook this

86

mixture thoroughly until it will leave the pan clean. Take it off the fire and add a little cayenne, finely chopped parsley, 4 oz. breadcrumbs, 2 oz. grated cheese, and 1 egg beaten in separately. When the mixture is quite cool roll it into balls with flour and fry them. Serve hot with a garnish of mashed potatoes. This dish is improved by thick brown sauce, for which a recipe follows.

THICK BROWN SAUCE (for recipe above)

Fry 1 onion, 1 lump of sugar and a little butter until quite brown, add 2 teaspoonfuls of wholemeal flour and ½ pint vegetable stock, with pepper and salt to taste. Boil well and strain.

Cheese Sauce

Place ½ pint milk in a pan and add a teaspoonful of corn-flour. Boil up, remove from cooker and beat in 3 oz. of grated cheese.

Cheese and Tomato Paste

Flake ½ lb. Cheddar cheese. Take 2 good-sized tomatoes and peel them (by placing in hot water for a few minutes). Put the tomatoes into a basin, chop and beat them into a pulp, add pepper and a little chopped parsley, mint and thyme. Mix the tomato pulp with the grated cheese and beat well together until a paste is produced. Press into small soufflé dishes.

This makes a grand filling for the small individual marrows such as Argentine and South African.

Swiss Croûte Fromage

6 oz. grated Gruyère cheese. 4 slices bread. 1 egg. ½ pint milk. Juice of ¼ lemon. ½ oz. butter.

Beat the egg in the milk, season with salt and pepper and a little lemon juice. Dip the bread slices in this mixture one at a time. Put alternate layers of soaked bread and grated cheese into a greased pie dish, ending with a layer of cheese. Pour the remaining milk over the dish, dot with butter and bake in a moderate oven for 20 minutes.

Swiss Fondue

¾ lb. Gruyère cheese. ½ pint milk. 2 oz. butter. 1 clove garlic finely chopped. ½ bottle white wine.

Slice the cheese and melt it in the milk over a gentle heat until the mixture begins to thicken. Season with salt and pepper. Add the wine and the garlic (previously simmered together for 10 minutes). Stir in the butter in small pieces. Serve with French bread.

Swiss Eggs

½ lb. Gruyère cheese. 4 eggs. 1 gill cream. Salt, pepper, butter.

Butter a shallow fireproof dish. Line with slices of cheese. Break the eggs into the dish, keeping them whole. Season the cream with salt and pepper and pour it over the eggs. Sprinkle with grated cheese. Bake in a moderate oven for 10 minutes.

CHAPTER 11

Brewer's Yeast

This is the smallest of cultivated plants, about the size of a human blood corpuscle. It is grown in huge vats until it has produced the greatest possible number of yeast cells. After the waste materials have been separated it is dried and then ground to powder and made into compressed tablets for human consumption.

It is a very rich source of vitamin B, with *all* the elements of the B complex, and it has a large amount of protein containing the substances necessary for digestion and assimilation. Its content of vitamin B, for example, is conclusive evidence of its usefulness. While 4 oz. of beans contain up to 600 parts of B_1, and liver about 400 parts, brewer's yeast has up to 8,000 parts. The vitamin B_2 content is just as impressive. When it is realised that the consumption of sugar and alcohol uses up large quantities of the essential vitamin B and that owing to the quantities of over-refined foods consumed there is often a big deficiency of vitamin B group in one's normal diet, the value of brewer's yeast tablets will be understood.

Choline and inositol, for instance, are two elements of the vitamin B complex that combat arterio-sclerosis and its attendant ailments.

J. I. Rodale, in *The Health Finder*, tells of an interesting experiment started about 25 years ago to see if brewer's yeast would combat cancer. The tests were carried out at the Sloan-Kettering Institute for Cancer Research. It was found that an artificial substance used to colour margarine and butter substitutes, known as butter yellow, could produce cancer in the liver of rats *within* 150 *days*. Incidentally, this product is now banned by law. Mixed with rice it was a certain producer of cancer in the liver of rats.

Rice was chosen as it is the staple food of India, China, Japan and the Orient generally. In Japan and Korea liver cancer comprises about 45% of all cancers. Brown rice has a riboflavin (vitamin B_2) content of only $\frac{1}{2}$ mg. per gram, while brewer's yeast has about 70 mg. and yeast has some 49% protein as against only 8% in rice.

Four groups of rats were put on a cancer-encouraging diet of butter yellow and rice. In addition, one of these groups was fed 3% brewer's yeast, another 6% and a third 15%. The fourth control group had no addition. The result was that all the control animals developed liver cancer within the 150 days, and *none* of the rats that had the 15% addition of brewer's yeast developed cancer. The other two groups had varying results, some developing cancer and others cirrhosis of the liver. But the experiment proved scientifically and conclusively that the inclusion of as little as 15% yeast prevented cancer. Various other experiments were conducted and the earlier results could not be shaken.

I agree that these were tests carried out on animals and that the results might not be the same in human beings, but as Dr. Sugiura, of the Sloan-Kettering Institute, says: "These dietary influences may prove to play a very large part in the causation, prevention and treatment of human cancer." In other words a diet rich in the vitamins and proteins contained in brewer's yeast will go very far towards protecting the body against the onset of carcinoma of any kind. I would emphasise that this is not *my* opinion; I give here the actual facts of an experiment, which is on record, by serious and qualified workers.

Now having said all this about brewer's yeast, I want it

to be clearly understood that it is no more a wonder food and a panacea for all the ills than anything else, and too much can be made of it if pursued to excess, just as with molasses. It is a grand food, and has all the elements that make for health if taken in moderation.

It must be remembered that yeast is very rich in protein and the protein is very concentrated. As has been shown, it is a very potent source of all the vitamin B complex group. Compare the content of 4 oz. of liver at 400 parts against that of yeast at 8,000 parts for a similar weight. Furthermore, yeast has not one or two of the B complex vitamins, but the whole lot and, like everything else in Nature, in the correct proportions.

The great thing in correct feeding is balance, as in everything else for that matter. Many people who live a regular life on a rational diet, which of course includes wholewheat bread, can do without any yeast at all. Especially if their intake of sugar—refined or otherwise—and alcohol is limited. But if they absorb a quantity of these then they need something like yeast to remedy the vitamin B deficiency from which they will suffer.

Brewer's yeast can be obtained in small compressed tablets very easy to swallow and no harm can ensue if these are taken daily. I must mention that the yeast protein is short on one of the amino acids called methionine, and the lack of this can be corrected by adding wholewheat bread. Lest it be concluded that the protein in yeast is a complete food I may mention that experiments on rats showed that animals fed on a diet of which the sole source of protein was yeast became entirely sterile. Once again rats are not human beings, but this does emphasise the need for *balance*.

To sum up, brewer's yeast is a most excellent and reliable source of natural vitamin B, containing all the B complex. It is not a good source of vitamin A. It is very high indeed in *vegetable* protein, so high in fact that it should be taken in moderation mixed with other protein-containing foods. In this connection it should be emphasised that vegetable proteins are alkaline in their reactions and although they do not contain every one of the twenty or so varieties of the amino acids that are in animal proteins, which are acid forming, they are much to be preferred.

Brewer's yeast is safe for those who are slimming. It contains no fats, starch, or sugar, and so is quite a suitable ingredient of diet for diabetics. But the point must be made that an excess of protein, while doing no good, is not harmful, and will not be converted into fat in the body as will an excess of carbohydrates.

Try these two yeast recipes. The Yeast Cake is from Poland, and the Fried Yeast Cakes (*Gebackene Mäuse*) are an Austrian delicacy.

Yeast Cake

1 lb. flour. 3 oz. sugar. 3 oz. butter. 4 eggs. 2 oz. sultanas. ½ pint milk. 2 oz. yeast. Salt. Grated lemon peel. Icing sugar.

Dissolve the yeast in a little warm milk. Mix the flour, sugar and a good pinch of salt in a bowl. Add 3 beaten eggs and the yeast. Knead until smooth. Soften the butter and add it and the sultanas to the dough. Half fill a greased baking tin with the dough and leave in a warm place until the dough rises to double its size. Glaze with a little beaten egg. Bake in a hot oven for 40 minutes. Cover thinly with icing sugar.

Fried Yeast Cakes (*Gebackene Mäuse*)

½ lb. flour. 2 oz. butter. ⅛th pint milk (approx.). 1 egg (beaten). ½ oz. yeast. ½ oz. sugar. 2 oz. sultanas. ½ teaspoonful salt. 1 tablespoonful rum. Vegetable fat for frying.

Scald the milk with the butter and cool to lukewarm. Cream the yeast with the sugar and stand it in a warm place for 5 minutes. Warm the flour in a large mixing bowl. Make a well in the flour and, using the hand, gradually beat in the egg, yeast mixture, milk mixture, salt and sultanas. Knead thoroughly. Cover the bowl with a cloth and stand it in a warm place for the mixture to rise. When the dough has doubled its bulk, in about an hour and a half, knock down lightly. Scoop out teasponfuls of the dough and fry in deep hot fat. Turn the " buns " to brown evenly on both sides. Drain on soft paper and serve hot with vanilla cream (as follows).

VANILLA CREAM

½ pint milk. 1 large egg. 2 oz. sugar. 1 oz. cornflour. 1 vanilla pod cut into 4 or 5 pieces, or drops of vanilla essence to taste.

Mix the cornflour, sugar and egg yolk to a paste with a little of the milk. Heat the remainder of the milk with the vanilla pod in a double saucepan. Pour the hot milk over the other ingredients, stirring all the time. When blended cook, stirring until thick.

CHAPTER 12

Yogurt

I am indebted to Mr. Gilbert Harris of Rugby, the owner of the Khormaksar herd of dairy goats, who exports his yogurt products all over the world, for a number of facts regarding yogurt and also for a number of most excellent recipes.

I would say at the beginning that I cannot too strongly advocate the continued use of yogurt for health. But—it must be yoghourt made by incubating two bacteria, *L.B. Bulgaricus* and *S. Thermophilus*, in high quality milk at the right temperature and for the correct length of time. If the temperature is too high the bacteria die; if too low they don't breed: if incubation is too short all of the milk is not converted; if too long, the bacteria become overcrowded and die.

The milk it is made from is also very important. *Ex nihilo nihil fit*—if you don't put it down you can't pick it up. Just as the quality of the vegetable is determined by the quality of the soil in which it grows, so is yogurt governed by the quality of the milk used. Frequently it is made from cow's milk—generally, I should say—but the finest and safest is made from goat's milk.

I know that cows in Britain are reckoned to be T.T. but goats have never been tested—they don't get tuberculosis at all, and their milk is easily digested in one tenth the time of cow's milk. Not infrequently, " curdled " milk is labelled as yogurt, which it is not. Neither is " sour " milk yogurt, and if this sour milk is sour pasteurised milk it should never be consumed. It will be putrid rather than sour, because the milk was practically dead to begin with and all kinds of dangerous toxins will be set up by the putrefying bacteria.

Mr. Gilbert Harris also makes the point that koumiss and keffir milk are not true yogurt either. Being prepared with floral cultures that look like little pieces of cauliflower, these products have quite different therapeutic effects.

Inevitably, there is a " synthetic " starter, made commercially by chemical companies. It is nothing like as good as the real natural culture, but of course it acts much more quickly, is cheaper and saves time—and makes money. It is very like yogurt but, just as chemists cannot make a complete vitamin, or a fertiliser maker cannot introduce the correct proportion of " trace " elements into his product, so there is " something " lacking in the synthetic starter. This " yogurt " won't keep longer than a day or so, while the natural variety, properly capped, will keep perfectly for at least fourteen days and up to a month, the reason being that the bacteria are still alive and act as a natural preservative.

One great advantage of yogurt which has recently been discovered is that it has an instant effect on the intestines after a course of the penicillin and sulphonamide drugs. It is being used extensively for this purpose and it also works wonders in curing stomach ulcers, especially in conjunction with a herbal treatment. Like the herbal treatment, it cannot cause any damage however much is consumed.

As it's name implies, the *B. Bulgaricus* is of Balkan origin, and it is well known that in Bulgaria there is a higher percentage of centenarians among the peasantry than anywhere else. Of course it is not all due to yogurt but to the general natural way of life, but yogurt has helped.

There is no maximum quantity that may be consumed; the more you eat the better will be your health. Taken regularly it will be a great slimming agent and will also build up deficiencies in lean flesh and muscle.

I am indebted to Mr. Harris for a number of the following most excellent recipes from many lands, using yogurt. They are most nourishing and uncommon. Yogurt makes an excellent salad dressing without any preparation. Mix it with raw fruit juice and freeze it in the refrigerator and it is a wonderful summer sweet.

Bazillah Soup (Arabia)

1 cup dried peas. 1 tablespoonful stock. 1 small onion. 1 tablespoonful fat and 1 of flour. 1 pint water. ½ pint yogurt. Sprig of parsley. Salt.

Soak peas overnight. Boil them in the water and soup stock with the onion, chopped parsley and salt until cooked. Make a light binding of the flour and fat, add to the soup, bring slowly to the boil and cook for half an hour. When ready to serve, add the yogurt and serve with fried bread croutons.

Ghali Ruzz Soup (Arabia)

Made as above, using rice instead of peas.

These are two delightful soups with a truly captivating oriental flavour.

Galushka Testa (Balkans)

A Balkan garnishing to add to any soup.

½ egg. 1 teaspoonful flour. 1 tablespoonful yogurt. Nut of margarine. Salt.

Mix all together into a light batter and pour very slowly into the boiling soup.

Zibdi Tomatoes (Arabia)

Tomatoes. 2 tablespoonfuls yogurt. 2 tablespoonfuls bread crumbs. 2 oz. grated cheese. Salt and pepper.

Cut a slice off the top of each tomato, scoop out the insides and mix together with the other ingredients. Stuff the tomatoes with the mixture and place in a greased dish in a fairly hot oven for 15 minutes.

Chestnut Salsah (Spain)

1 lb. chestnuts. ½ pint yogurt. 2 tablespoonfuls white wine, (can be omitted). 1 teaspoonful flour. Nut of butter.

Boil chestnuts until soft, remove inner and outer skins and put nuts through the mincer. Add yoghourt, wine, flour and butter. Work it well together and cook slowly, stirring all the time.

This is an intriguing sauce to add to any savoury dish.

Anillo Leopoldina (Italy)

6 oz. mashed potatoes. 1 egg. ½ pint yogurt. 1 teaspoonful flour. 1 oz. margarine. Salt.

Mix the mashed potatoes, yogurt, egg yolk and flour together and beat well to make a light mixture. Make a ring of mixture inside a well-greased dish and put in the oven to brown at a medium heat. Serve your savoury or meat dishes inside the ring.

Lebanon Beans

1 lb. French beans. 1 oz. fat. 1 tablespoonful flour.
2 tablespoonfuls yogurt. Chopped parsley. ½ teaspoonful sugar. A little salt.

Cut up the beans and place in a saucepan with the fat,
three tablespoonfuls of water, parsley, sugar and salt.
Cook slowly with the lid on, until tender. Sprinkle the
flour on the beans, add a little water and bring to the boil.
Allow to simmer for a few minutes. Add the yogurt and
boil up for a minute or so before serving.

Yoghourt Mayonnaise (Balkans)

1 oz. butter. 1 oz. flour. ½ pint milk. ½ pint yogurt.
1 egg yolk. 1 tablespoonful sugar. 1 teaspoonful French
mustard. Juice of ½ lemon. Salt to taste.

Melt butter, remove from heat and stir in flour. Replace
on heat, add milk and stir constantly until it thickens.
Take off heat and add yolk of egg while still hot, then mix
in lemon juice, one tablespoonful sugar, a little salt, the
mustard, and lastly the yogurt. Allow to cool before
use. This can be bottled and kept in a cool place or
refrigerator.

Banana Salad (U.S.A.)

2 bananas. 1 lettuce. 2 oz. chopped walnuts. 1 orange.
Yogurt.

Skin the bananas and slit lengthways. Arrange them on a
bed of lettuce. Cover with yogurt and sprinkle with

chopped walnuts. Peel and quarter the orange and arrange between banana slices.

California Salad (U.S.A.)

¼ cucumber. 2 apples. 2 bananas. 3 tomatoes. 1 lettuce. Salt, pepper, lemon juice and yogurt.

Dice the cucumber, slice thinly the apples, bananas and tomatoes. Sprinkle cucumber and tomatoes with salt and pepper. Squeeze lemon juice over the apples and bananas. Arrange on a bed of lettuce and cover lightly with fresh yogurt.

Beigl (Hungary)

½ lb. flour. 3 oz. butter. 1 egg yolk. 1 tablespoonful rum (can be omitted). 2 tablespoonfuls yogurt. ½ pint milk. ½ lb. ground almonds. ½ lb. sugar. ¾ tablespoonful sultanas. Pinch of yeast.

Make pastry from butter, flour, egg yolk, yogurt, pinch of yeast and rum. Allow to stand whilst the filling is prepared. Make a syrup of sugar and milk, add the almonds and cook on a slow heat for a few minutes, stirring continuously. Remove from heat, add nut of butter and sultanas and allow filling to cool. Roll out the pastry very thinly, cut into two halves and place half of the filling into each. Roll them up and put into a greased tin. Brush the tops with egg white. Allow to stand for ten minutes then put into hot oven and cook for 40 minutes.

Beigl can be kept for a long time in an airtight tin.

Silesian Pancakes (Russia)

2 oz. butter. ¼ pint yogurt. ¼ pint milk. 2 oz. sugar.
2 oz. flour. 2 eggs. Jam.

Cream butter and sugar, add eggs one at a time with a
little flour, then fold in the rest of the flour. Mix the milk
and yogurt and warm slightly and stir in. Half fill
greased patty tins and bake in a moderate oven for 10 to
15 minutes. Turn out on to sugar-sprinkled board and
sandwich together with a little hot jam.

Zabaglione Flan (Portugal)

¼ pint milk. ¼ pint yogurt. 2 oz. castor sugar. 2 eggs.
3 tablespoonfuls sherry. Fresh fruit.

Make a pastry flan case. Heat milk and yogurt to blood
heat. Whisk egg yolk and sugar until light, and mix milk
and yogurt in with whisk. Stand bowl over boiling
water and beat mixture until it is thick. Remove from
heat and stir in sherry. Allow to cool and beat in stiffly
whisked egg whites. Spread a layer of the mixture over the
flan case and cover with fresh strawberries, raspberries,
cherries, peaches or apricots, or a mixture of fresh fruits.
Cover over with the rest of the mixture and decorate with
a little of the fresh fruit.

Crêpe Indie (West Indies)

4 tablespoonfuls flour. ¼ pint milk. ¼ pint yogurt.
1 teaspoonful rum or brandy (can be omitted). 1 egg.
2 oz. butter. 2 tablespoonfuls sultanas. 1 tablespoonful
Barbados sugar.

Mix flour, milk, y o g u r t, rum, egg yolk and sultanas into a thick pancake batter. Heat butter in a frying pan and pour in sufficient batter for individual portions; turn to brown on both sides. Serve hot, sprinkled with Barbados sugar and a little jam on the side.

Gulyas Leves (Hungary)

1 tablespoonful fat. 1 onion, 1 carrot, 1 parsnip, 1 tomato (all medium-sized). 1 teaspoonful paprika. 4 oz. meat. Caraway seeds. Salt. 1 pint water. ½ pint y o g u r t.

Melt fat in saucepan, chop onions and fry till lightly browned. Turn heat low and add sliced carrot, parsnip and tomato. Cut meat into small cubes and add to mixture with salt and a few caraway seeds. Stir for a few minutes, then add water and bring to the boil. Simmer until meat is half cooked, add one or two diced potatoes and cook till tender. Add the y o g u r t and serve straight away.

This is a nourishing meal for a cold day.

Sharos (Greece)

1 egg. ½ pint y o g u r t. ½ pint milk. 1½ tablespoonfuls Barbados sugar. 1½ tablespoonfuls currants or sultanas.

Beat egg well and mix into milk and y o g u r t. Beat again, adding sugar and then the fruit. Cook in a slow oven until firm.

Curd Caramel Crisp (Greece)

4 oz. sugar. ¼ pint y o g u r t. ½ pint milk. 2 eggs. 3 oz. bread cut into half-inch cubes. 4 tablespoonfuls water.

101

Dissolve sugar in water and boil quickly until it forms caramel. Take off heat for a few minutes and slowly add a further 4 tablespoonfuls of water and re-boil. Grease a dish, put in the diced bread, pour the caramel over it and leave to soak. Beat the eggs, bring milk to the boil and pour into eggs, stirring rapidly. Break up the curd as small as possible and mix in the yogurt. Pour over the bread and leave for 15 minutes. Bake in slow oven for 25 minutes, until custard has set.

Barth Curd Cake (Germany)

Cake: 3 oz. butter. 2 oz. icing sugar. 1 egg yolk. 4 oz. S.R. flour. 2 tablespoonfuls milk.
Curd: ½ pint yogurt. 2 egg yolks. 3 egg whites. ½ oz. butter. 2 oz. castor sugar. Vanilla essence.

Grease, and line with greased paper, an 8- or 9-inch tin with loose base. Cream butter and sugar and mix in un-beaten egg yolk lightly. Stir in flour gradually and mix with milk to stiff consistency. Spread in tin and bake in moderate heat until pale gold. Meanwhile put yogurt into basin and with wooden spoon stir in unbeaten egg yolks, soft butter and castor sugar. Blend well and add vanilla essence (or currants, grated orange and lemon rinds, or chopped almonds). Beat three egg whites stiff and fold in. When base is cooked, cover with curd and return to cook for a further 15 minutes at increased heat. Serve hot or cold.

CHAPTER 13

Mushrooms

In my opinion they are among the most delectable of vegetables, and are excellent for imparting a flavour to almost any meal. They contain protein to the extent of 4·3% and are very low in fat, only ·3%, while they contain B_1 vitamin in the ratio of 100 I.U.'s per 7 oz.—not a lot of anything, but more than many others. For example, it takes at least 25 oz. of cheese to provide 100 units of vitamin B_1.

A few facts may be of interest. The cultivated mushroom is considered the best, but in Belgium, France, Germany and Russia there are several varieties known, which are highly prized. In general they have perhaps a more delicate flavour, but it takes an expert (or a native of the country) to distinguish them from a highly poisonous variety of fungus. It is safer to buy the British type, in a shop. The cultivation of the mushroom has rapidly increased of recent years and is now a very big business. It is not a job for the uninitiated, as it requires a good deal of skill, unremitting attention and knowledge.

Mushroom flavouring adds a delightful taste to a large number of dishes, and if mushroom powder is made this is available all the year round from the storeroom cupboard. (The recipe is given on page 105.)

There are a great many uses for mushrooms—on toast as a savoury; in an omelette; with oysters; with chicken; with tomatoes; stuffed with bacon; with fish; with garlic, thyme, marjoram and parsley; or used as a

103

stuffing for chicken (with oysters). They are excellent when pickled and everyone is familiar with mushroom ketchup, which is very easy to make at home and far better than the bought variety. Preserved in Oil of Madeira or tomato pulp they are a grand standby for emergency meals. They are among the most useful of vegetables.

In the woods and hedgerows of Britain there are many varieties of fungi, some of which, notably the bright yellow Chanterelles are very good eating with a delicate flavour, but others particularly the Amanita species, the Fly Agaric (*Amanita muscaria*) which everyone must have seen, with bright red tops spotted white, are deadly poison. Space does not permit of a detailed description of edible and poisonous fungi and in any event this is done better by coloured illustrations. I would refer all interested to a work published by Macmillan—*Mushrooms and Toadstools,* by Dr. John Ramsbottom. This book, one of Collins New Naturalist Series, has no less than 84 full colour photographs and 58 black and white, and anyone who after having read this book goes out and gathers and eats poisonous fungi has deliberately committed suicide. And now for some mushroom recipes.

MUSHROOM RECIPES

Mushroom Cream

Cook 1 lb. of peeled mushrooms in 2½ oz. of butter or vegetable margarine until tender, then take off the heat. Add a tablespoonful of flour with seasoning (salt, pepper, allspice) and a tablespoonful of chopped parsley and 2 medium-sized tomatoes.

Mix 2 egg yolks with ½ pt. cream or evaporated milk.

Pour this into the saucepan, mix thoroughly and put on the fire again to heat but not to boil. Serve hot with thin crisp toast.

French Roll Mushrooms

Cook mushrooms required in butter or vegetable margarine and a little tomato juice.

Take the number of round French rolls required (the brown ones are delicious for this), scoop out the soft part and dip the hollow rolls into deep very hot fat for a few minutes, then drain.

Alternatively, moisten the inside of the roll with a little butter from the mushrooms and a little milk and put in the oven until very hot. Then fill the rolls with the mushrooms and garnish with a tomato ring.

Dried Mushrooms

Mushrooms can be dried in a cool oven. Small mushrooms can be dried whole but large ones should be peeled; the stalks removed, and cut in thick slices.

Once they are dried, mushroom powder can be made, and this is a very useful standby for imparting mushroom flavour to sauces, soups and stews. Pound the dried mushrooms in a mortar and rub through a sieve. Store in a cool dry place in airtight jars.

Mushroom Rice

Fry two chopped onions in 2 oz. of vegetable margarine. Add 6 more oz. margarine (or butter, of course) and $\frac{1}{2}$ lb. rice. Stir frequently until most of butter is absorbed. Then add 2 tablespoonfuls of chopped almonds, 2 bay leaves and a sprig of chopped thyme. Just cover this with boiling water and cook slowly until the rice is tender. Drain and mix with $\frac{3}{4}$ lb. mushrooms previously cooked. Put in a moderate oven for 5 minutes to let the moisture evaporate from the rice.

The mushrooms should be cooked previously by boiling rapidly for 5 minutes in 9 tablespoonfuls of water to which has been added a pinch of salt, the juice of half a lemon and 1 oz. butter. Drain when rice is ready.

Mushroom Ketchup No. I

7 lbs. of freshly gathered ripe mushrooms. ½ lb. salt. ½ oz. black pepper. ¼ teaspoonful pounded mace. ¼ oz. allspice. ½ oz. ginger. 2 oz. peeled shallots. 2 cloves garlic. 3 or 4 bay leaves. 6 cloves, to each quart of liquor.

Break the mushrooms in small pieces, put them in an earthenware pan and strew with the salt. Cover with a cloth and let stand until the following day. Then strain off the liquor, measure it and boil for 15 minutes. Add the seasonings and simmer for another 20 minutes. When quite cold put into dry bottles which have been washed in brandy, and seal tightly.

Mushroom Ketchup No. 2

Put a layer of large full-grown ripe mushrooms in the bottom of a deep earthen pan and sprinkle them with salt, then add another layer of mushrooms and another layer of salt, and so on alternately to the top of the pan, finishing with salt. Let the mushrooms stand for two or three hours, by which time the salt will have penetrated the mushrooms and rendered them easy to break. Then pound them with a mortar or mash them and let them stand for two days—not longer—stirring and mashing them well each day.

Then pour the pulp into a stone jar and to each quart add 1 oz. of whole black pepper. Stopper the jar very tightly and set it in a stewpan of boiling water and keep it boiling for two hours at least.

Take out the jar and pour the juice clear from the settlings through a hair sieve (without squeezing) into a clean stewpan and let it boil very gently for half an hour. Skim well and pour into a clean dry jar. Cover this tightly and let it stand in a cool place until next day, then pour off as gently as possible, so as not to disturb the settlings at the bottom of the jar, through a thick flannel bag until it is perfectly clear. Add a tablespoonful of brandy to each pint of ketchup and let it stand as before. A fresh sediment will be deposited from which the ketchup should be gently poured off and bottled in dry bottles which have been washed in brandy or spirits. Take especial care that the bottles are closely corked and sealed.

This is a good deal of trouble, but the result, if it has been carefully made, is well worth while.

Mushroom Soup

This is a foreign recipe. Put ½ lb. mushrooms in a saucepan with 1 tablespoonful of butter and sprinkle with 1 tablespoonful of paprika. Simmer very slowly for 10 or 15 minutes but without browning. Then add 1 tablespoonful of flour and stir until the flour is lightly coloured. Add gradually, stirring continuously, 2 pints of boiling vegetable stock (see page 136), bring to the boil and simmer for one hour. A few minutes before serving beat in the yolk of 1 egg with 6 tablespoonfuls of y o g u r t or sour cream, add 2 or 3 tablespoonfuls of the hot stock, and when well mixed add this to the soup and stir but do not allow to boil.

Mushrooms and Tomatoes

For each 1 lb. of mushrooms allow ½ lb. of tomatoes. Peel the mushrooms and quarter them. Quarter the tomatoes. Put the mushrooms and tomatoes in a well-buttered fireproof dish, sprinkle with 1 teaspoonful of chopped shallot or onion, 1 oz. parsley, the juice of ½ a lemon, and season with salt and pepper. Sprinkle with 1 or 2 tablespoonfuls of olive oil and bake in a quick oven for 20 minutes or longer according to the size of the mushrooms.

Pickled Mushrooms

Wash and dry the mushrooms thoroughly and remove the stalks. Pack them closely in jars, add a few bay leaves, a few shallots or cloves of garlic (if liked) and cover with boiling vinegar. Let stand until quite cold and seal tightly.

Mushrooms as a Garnish

This is a standard recipe. Choose mushrooms as nearly as possible of the same size. Wash them in cold water, but never let them stand in water. Dry them thoroughly, remove stalks and peel. For every ½ lb. of mushrooms allow 6 tablespoonfuls of water, 1 heaped salt spoon of salt, the juice of ½ a lemon and 1 oz. of butter. Bring the salted water and the lemon juice to the boil, add the mushrooms and then the butter. Boil rapidly for 4 minutes and the mushrooms are now ready for use. Remove from the fire and leave in the saucepan until required. They can then be drained and added to a sauce.

Mushrooms can be prepared in this manner the day before they are needed and kept in an earthenware casserole with the liquid and covered with buttered paper. To retain their full flavour, mushrooms should always be cooked in a small quantity of liquid and boiled rapidly. A common mistake is to add mushrooms to a sauce or stew and let them cook too long. They become tough and lose their flavour. When cooked in the manner of this garnish they can be added to the sauce, etc., only a few minutes before serving.

Mushrooms Marinated

Cook small mushrooms as for a garnish. Drain, and when cold pack them closely in jars, with air-tight lids, with 1 or 2 cloves of garlic, 2 or 3 bay leaves, a few sprigs of fennel, peppercorns and salt. Cover with cold boiled vinegar, pour a little olive oil on the top and screw on the lid. These are popular as a winter salad with a French salad dressing consisting of 2 tablespoonfuls of salad oil (preferably sunflower) to 1 tablespoonful of (preferably wine) vinegar, and a seasoning of salt and pepper.

Mushroom Stuffing

Choose small mushrooms, peel them and wipe them with a cloth. Chop them and cook them in a little butter, seasoning with salt, a dash of cayenne and a light sprinkling of mace. Mix with half their weight of breadcrumbs and stir well over a slow fire. Bind with one or two eggs, add a teaspoonful of grated lemon rind and a squeeze of lemon juice.

Mushroom and Oyster Stuffing
(For turkey and chicken)

Melt 1 oz. butter with the same quantity of oil in a saucepan. Add 1 tablespoonful of finely-chopped onion and 1 of chopped shallots. Then add ½ lb. of finely chopped mushroom stalks and peelings, previously well squeezed in a cloth so as to extract as much moisture as possible. Mix all thoroughly and cook until all moisture has completely evaporated from the mushrooms. To every 4 oz. add 2 oz.

of soft bread soaked in milk and dried in a saucepan over a quick heat and allowed to stand until cold. Put in a pan with a little butter, mix thoroughly and add a few oysters. Season highly with salt, pepper and a squeeze of lemon juice.

CHAPTER 14

Amateur Winemaking

A book on health foods would not, in my opinion, be complete without some mention of home winemaking, but this is a big subject and only the bare outlines can be given here.

There are some excellent companies catering for the needs of the home brewer. A beginner's outfit comprising everything necessary to make a start can be bought for as little at $5.25, and it is an absorbing hobby. I would emphasize, of course, that this is not a commercial matter.

Some years ago, before I left Cornwall, we had a tremendous crop of apples and, owing to the fine weather, there was also a great yield of honey, so we decided to make some wine with our surplus apples and honey. I have a first-class electric juice extractor and we got to work. A local friend of mine was an enthusiastic expert and had all the equipment. His account of his introduction to the art of winemaking was interesting. When in East Africa he had a hedge of pomegranates, the pips of which he pressed and filled a bottle with the juice. It fizzed, blew the cork out, and turned a muddy-looking mess. He replaced the cork lightly and put the bottle away on a shelf and forgot about it. A year later he took it out and found a clear, bright red liquid, on a sediment of mud, which drank like nectar—the clear liquid, not the mud! And he has been making his own wines ever since.

Wines can be made from the juice of almost every fruit and vegetable. Very simply, the way we did it was to make a gallon of apple juice with my electric juice extractor, lace it with honey and add a yeast " starter."

You can buy the type of yeast you require from several firms in Britain and a list of these appears in Appendix C. Many types of yeast are now available. For mead you will require a Maury culture (yeast made from grapes grown in Maury, S.E. France), and for sherry type, a sherry culture: also available are port, Malaga, Haut Sauterne, Liebfraumilch, Burgundy and others. A variety of bases are also procurable, to save the trouble of juicing at home —grape juice; apple juice; pear juice. They are all good.

I have not the space to describe fully the whole operation, fermenting the sweetened juice (the " must ") and feeding the yeast. Leave the mixture alone for some time, until fermentation has ceased, which can take about three months. Then carefully decant it and lightly cork the jar. And the longer it remains the better it becomes. The wine we made three years ago is just now maturing nicely. Made from apple juice, honey and yeast, it is a thoroughly healthy beverage, with minerals and half a dozen vitamins in the honey, lashings of vitamin B in the yeast, and potassium, calcium, sulphur and other minerals plus vitamin C in the apple. It is a real health drink, and very pleasant withal. It is also cheap, especially if you grow your own fruit and keep bees. We made two gallons and I regret that I have not had the time to make any more since I came to Scotland.

Very excellent wines can also be made at home from vegetables. The procedure is more or less the same. Juice the medium, add sugar (I prefer honey always as a sweetener and fermenter with yeast) and the yeast type required.

Rhubarb is a well-known wine, and so is parsnip. Both can be very potent. Carrot wine is excellent and so is parsley, but this also is very strong. I remember a friend who had served in the 1914 war in East Africa telling me that they arrived in a village which had been a German headquarters, and being the vanguard of the troops they had time to look around. They came upon a hut marked with a Red Cross, and inside were several bottles labelled " U. BOOT WHISKEY." Not having had a drink for a long time they settled in the evening for a " sundowner." In fact they had several, since the stuff seemed so mild. In the middle of the night they wakened, hearts going like sledge hammers, and they very nearly died. Upon inquiring from the local natives what the stuff was they were informed it was *Tembo ya Ndizi*—banana spirit—which was normally taken highly diluted. They had drunk bottles of it neat!

Many herbs make excellent wine with great health-giving properties, for example, balm wine, clary wine, coltsfoot wine, elderberry wine, and of course sloe wine and, most potent of all, sloe gin.

By far the best introduction to the craft of winemaking at home is the book written by H. E. Bravery: *Successful Wine Making at Home,* Arc , 95 cents. It contains literally everything you need to know. Here are Mr. Bravery's instructions for making typical country wines:

ELDER FLOWER WINE

1 *gal. flower*, 1 *gal. water*, 3½ *lb. sugar*, 1 *oz. yeast*, 2 *lemons*.

Boil half the sugar in half a gallon of water and while boiling pour over the flowers in the fermenting vessel. Add the juice of the lemons and when the mixture is cool add the yeast. Cover as directed and ferment for seven days.

Strain out the flowers and wring out well, but not too dry. Put the strained liquor in a gallon jar.

Boil the rest of the sugar and water for two minutes and when cool add to the rest. Cover as directed or fit fermentation lock and leave until all fermentation has ceased.

Another very good elder flower wine may be made in exactly the same way as the above using only five pints of the flowers with three pounds of sugar, two lemons, 1 oz. yeast and one gallon water.

ROSE PETAL WINE

One of the most delightful of all flower wines. The petals of roses of various colours may be used in one lot of wine, but if you have enough of, say, both red and yellow for a separate lot of each, do keep them separate.

3 *qts rose petals* (*strongly scented if possible*), 1 *gal. water*, 3 *lb. sugar*, 1 *oz. yeast*, 2 *lemons*.

Pour half a gallon of boiling water over the petals in the fermenting vessel, cover well and leave for forty-eight hours, stirring often.

Boil half the sugar in a quart of water for two minutes and when this is cool add to the petal mixture and ferment for three days.

Strain and wring out well, and return the liquor to the fermenting vessel and let it ferment for a further ten days.

Pour the liquor into a gallon jar, leaving as much of the deposit behind as you can. Then boil the rest of the sugar and water as before and when cool add to the rest together with the juice of the lemons. Cover again as directed or fit fermentation lock and leave until all fermentation has ceased.

(Full instructions are, of course, given in the book about racking, yeasts and nutrient.)

CHAPTER 15

Organic Fertilisers

Before beginning to discuss the growing and characteristics of the various culinary and salad herbs I think that some remarks on fertilizers, and the superiority of organic to artificial or chemical manures, are necessary. Here again it is a case of working with Nature.

Just as we have seen in the Vitamin chapter of this book there is always that " something " that eludes a manufacturer, so the makers of chemical fertilisers cannot possibly reproduce in their correct proportions the essential trace elements which go to make up the good earth.

I will grant that these artificial manures give an almost instant uplift to plants and crops. So does a strychnine heart tonic to a human being, but it does not last and the dose must be repeated. It is the same in medicine—you can get a quick reaction with a drug, but for a slow certain cure there is nothing to compare with a herbal treatment. But generally it is slow.

When a chemical fertiliser is applied it takes everything out of the ground and next year more of it is required. With an organic manure, which is made by returning the weeds and greenstuffs grown by the land back into the soil after having been composted, that which was taken from the earth for the process of growth is returned, and is readily absorbed again. Incidentally, chemicals kill worms, the greatest manure-makers of all.

I have ample proof of this. In Cornwall I bought a little country cottage which had been in the hands of an old Cornishman who was a keen gardener and who kept pigs. The little $\frac{1}{4}$-acre garden had been manured with well-rotted pig manure for generations, and the ground was so rich it would grow anything. When I removed to Scotland I acquired a garden that had once been good, but had later been laced with chemicals, with the result that the soil was useless for crops. It had developed club root, which was never there before, and the only things that grew were weeds. I hardly ever saw a worm anywhere. For a decade a succession of tenant gardeners had saturated the ground with all sorts of chemicals, raised good crops (in quantity) and then like the Arabs folded their tents and faded away. If ever I needed a lesson in manures, which I did not, I had it before me here. There was simply nothing left in the soil. I had it analysed, of course, but this was unnecessary; the poverty of the soil showed clearly in the crops.

We started making compost and using seaweed, the greatest manure known. For reference, I am giving (p. 117) full instructions on how to construct a compost heap; it is quite easy and very rewarding. This compost, when properly made, will contain everything that the soil requires, including the trace elements in the correct proportions.

This simply cannot be done artificially—consider only boron as an example. The quantity necessary (and it is entirely necessary) for growth is less than $\cdot0005\%$, and any excess of this figure will quite easily kill the plants. It sounds most incredible, but it is a proved fact that much less than $\cdot0005\%$ of one element alone is needed. Now the usual source of boron chemically is borax, and the top weight of borax necessary for an acre of ground is, say, 15 lbs. So the problem of the farmer using chemicals is to distribute 15 lbs. *evenly* over one whole acre—and it must be evenly; it is useless having an excess in one place and none in another.

That is only one trace element. Cobalt is a bigger head-ache. And then there is magnesium, and—but why go on? These are quite enough to emphasise that when a natural compost is available, which has everything in balance without trouble, it seems stupid to pay money for artificial elements, impoverish the soil, and chance getting a correct trace element mixture, the odds against which are colossal. It means for the small gardener, who thinks in yards, that he has to weigh out 1/20th oz. of borax, carefully mix it in some medium like fine soil or sand, and distribute this evenly over one yard of the selected ground. Then he wants all the other elements in varying proportions. It is not worth the labour. Even when this has been accomplished it is only an artificial product after all, and not to be compared with Mother Nature's.

I have stressed this point because I do feel very strongly on the matter. In growing a crop, obviously something is taken from the soil and absorbed into the plants, and the logical and natural way to put it back is to return all the greenstuff and add a quantity of well-rotted farmyard manure. It is more labour than just throwing a handful of powdered chemicals over the land but it pays every time.

Here then, is how to make a compost heap. First of all remember that the heap must be started on the ground and not on boards or a cement floor. A bottomless wooden bin of slats, set an inch apart to allow for ventilation, about 4 ft. square and 5 ft. high, will make about a ton of finished compost. Another excellent method is to arrange some strong posts in a 4-ft. square and run 4-in. or 6-in. mesh wire netting round to contain the material. This gives splendid ventilation.

Use all the garden refuse and kitchen waste, and everything else green such as grass clippings, all weeds, nettles (very good), seaweed of course in any quantity, sawdust, and any surplus straw or hay available. At least 20%

should consist of farmyard or animal manure of some kind. Sewage is excellent also.

Start off with a layer of the above, mixing the greenstuff and manure, about 6-8 ins. deep. Then sprinkle lightly with friable soil and apply a compost activator. There are numbers of these on the market and they are all good. Keep on with this sequence of layers until the bin or netting is full, and cover the top with about 2-3 ins. of soil. Then cover the heap with a board or sheets of corrugated iron to keep out the wind and rain. Don't soak the mass, but dry materials like sawdust, hay and straw should be dampened. If this heap has been properly prepared it should be ready in about two months, given suitably warm weather. In cooler conditions it will take longer.

This is the simplest form of a compost heap for small gardens. But a more elaborate, and consequently superior, type was devised by the late Sir Albert Howard, whose name is honoured in every circle connected with the soil. He evolved the Indore compost heap at the Indore Research Station in India. It consists of a series of layers of mixed vegetable matter with between them other layers of nitrogenous manure and others of chalk, limestone, earth or wood ash, as the neutraliser, or base.

When Sir Albert Howard (who died in 1944 at the age of 73 after years of service in India) originated the Indore Process, he laid down that there must be a certain amount of nitrogen as energy food for the bacteria in the heap. The green materials contain some but not enough, so added nitrogen is made by the addition of farmyard manure, urine, dried blood, etc. The Indore heap begins with roughly 30 parts of carbon (in woody matter) and carbohydrates to between 1 and 2 parts of nitrogen in the manure. Sir Albert also stressed that the heap must be lightly built and not packed hard, to allow for free aeration of the mass. This is most important; there *must* be a free circulation of air, and that is one reason why I like a heap made with wire netting walls.

It is not possible in this small book to go deeply into the subject of compost, but I hope that I have opened a new field of study to those of my readers who are desirous of acquiring more knowledge about the culture of the living soil. I cannot do better than suggest a course of reading of the works of Sir Albert Howard.

CHAPTER 16

Herbs for Health

> The Lord hath created medicines out of the earth,
> and he that is wise will not abhor them.
>   ECCLESIASTICUS XXXVIII 4.

As with many other great benefits conferred on mankind, we are indebted to Egypt for the origin of medical science. In the days of Moses Egyptian knowledge of medical science was famous.

Kheiron brought the knowledge from Egypt to Greece. His pupil Aesculapius carried on the good work and then came " The Father of Medicine," the colossal figure of Hippocrates. In his steps followed Celsus who wrote several books on medical science. After him Galen and then there was a lull in giant figures in the craft until at the beginning of the 16th century came Paracelsus, who was the first to introduce chemical formulae to the world. He was so contemptuous of Galen and his herbal remedies that he burnt his books and substituted his own ideas of the chemical mineral practice which has attained such proportions at the present day.

This Paracelsus contended that he had found the Elixir of Life that would prolong mortal existence indefinitely. It did not work in his case, for he died early, at fifty-one, while Galen lived to a good old age.

That great evangelist and herbalist John Wesley remarks that the healing art was first brought into use in a very natural manner in the earliest times, when the earth was young, and in the absence of chemists, commerce and advertising, man had to find out by trial and error the virtues, and dangers, of the various plants growing around him.

The Preacher declaimed sonorously that " The Lord hath created medicines out of the earth." It is for us to heed and take note. The medicines are all here waiting to be used, and we have now a considerable knowledge of *how* to use them. There is a herb or combination of herbs for almost every ill, but remember that the action of herbs is slow.

You can have a chemical to give what is now termed " a shot in the arm " which affords an immediate jerk to the system, but it does not last and the succeeding stage is worse than the beginning—just like the artificial fertilizer in the good earth.

In the following pages I enumerate many varieties of herbs, both culinary and medicinal, which are in daily use. Many can be grown in a cottage garden, especially the culinary varieties, and the medicinal types can be obtained readily at health food stores in tablets compounded in the correct proportions by a skilled herbal chemist to afford the best results.

There are, of course, many hundred varieties of useful herbs, but I shall endeavor to select the most important in each category. I personally grow the majority of the herbs which I list. As many of the descriptive terms may be unfamiliar to some readers, here are explanations of those which have been used:

Anthelmintic	Expelling or destroying worms.
Antiseptic	Preventing mortification.
Anti-spasmodic	Relieving spasms.
Aperient	Opening.
Aromatic	Agreeable—spicy.
Astringent	Contracting the fibres or solids.

Carminative	Expelling wind.
Demulcent	Softening, sheathing or lubricating.
Diaphoretic	Producing perspiration.
Diuretic	Increasing the discharge of urine.
Emollient	Softening, causing warmth and moisture.
Emmenagogic	Promoting menstruation.
Febrifugal	Dispelling fever, allaying fever heat.
Nervine	Strengthening the nerves.
Pectoral	Useful in diseases of the lungs and chest.
Refrigerant	Cooling, mitigating heat.
Sedative	Depressing the vital powers.
Stimulative	Exciting action-giving strength.
Stomachic	To excite the action of, and strengthen, the stomach.
Vermifugal	Destroying worms.

Angelica (*Angelica archangelica*)
>Stimulating, carminative, diuretic.

Medicinal: Infusion of 1 oz. herb to 1 pint boiling water
>Dose: 1 wineglassful frequently.

Culinary: Candied for use in cakes and confectionery.
Easily grown from seed or plants in any garden. Grows up to 6 ft. and flowers in second year, then dies. Excellent bee plant. Perennial if not allowed to flower.

Aniseed (*Pimpinella anisum*)
>Carminative and pectoral.

Medicinal: Used in cough medicines.
Culinary: Used as a condiment.
Grown from seed. Annual, 18 ins.

Balm (*Melissa officinalis*)
>Carminative, diaphoretic, febrifugal.

Medicinal: Balm tea made by pouring 1 pint boiling water
>on 1 oz. herb. Let it stand for ¼ hour, strain and drink

freely. Induces mild perspiration, and makes a pleasant cooling tea for feverish patients.

Culinary: Leaves used in salads. Sprig crushed in cider is excellent.

Grown easily from seed or plants in any garden. Perennial, spreads rapidly. 2½ ft.

Bush Basil (*Ocimum minimum*)

Aromatic, carminative, cooling.

Although generally employed for cooking and flavouring purposes, it has occasionally been used with success in medicine for mild nervous disorders.

Culinary: Leaves used in small quantities for flavouring soups, vinegars, fish, etc. Warm, clove-like flavour.

Grown in British gardens from seed. Sow thinly at end May in position. Plants do not like transplanting. Better plants are obtained by potting in greenhouse.

Bergamot (*Monardia didyma*)

Perennial, very ornamental with delicate aroma. Leaves and flowers used in salads, and leaves make a delightful addition to ordinary tea.

Grows freely from either seed or plants. Plants do best when split annually, keeping the younger roots and discarding the dead centre. Best in part shade. 3 ft.

Borage (*Borago officinalis*)

Diuretic, demulcent, emollient.

Annual, grows to 3 ft. with beautiful sky-blue flowers and black anthers. As the flowers face downwards, they are better seen in a high position.

Flowers and leaves are delicious in salads and the cucumber-flavoured leaves make a good sandwich filling, and add coolness to any drink, especially claret cup and Pimms No. 1. Used in France for fevers and pulmonary complaints (1 oz. leaves to 1 pint boiling water.) Also as poultice for inflammatory swellings.

Sow in September for flowers early spring. Seeds itself freely. Sow in March for summer flowering. Excellent bee plant.

Burnet (*Sanguisorba officinalis*)

Astringent, tonic, also used in hemorrhages.

Salad Burnet, a perennial, is a very pleasant ingredient in salads. Flavor somewhat like cucumber and borage. A wine was made from it in the old days.

Camomile (*Anthemis nobilis*)

Stomachic, anti-spasmodic, tonic.

An old-fashioned but extremely efficacious remedy for hysterical and nervous conditions in women. Also good as an emmenagogue.

The flowers combined with crushed poppy heads make a good poultice for allaying pains when other means have failed. Camomile tea, made from the flower heads, is excellent as a sedative before retiring to rest. Also makes a very good hair wash.

Grows easily from seed and transplants well. Makes an excellent lawn, hardwearing and aromatic. As Falstaff remarks—the more it is trodden on, the faster it grows. Perennial.

Caraway (*Carum carvi*)

Carminative, stimulant.

Used in children's ailments, flatulence and stomachic derangements, and as a flavouring for culinary uses.

Catnip, Catmint (*Nepeta cataria*)

Carminative, tonic, diaphoretic.

As it produces free perspiration, it is very useful in colds, etc. An infusion of the leaves, 1 oz. to 1 pint boiling water may be taken by adults in 2 tablespoonfuls, by children 2 or 3 teaspoonfuls, frequently, to relieve pain and flatulence.

Perennial, grows freely from seed or plants. 18 ins.

Cecily, Sweet Cecily (*Myrrhis odorata*)
Carminative, expectorant.

The fresh root may be eaten freely. It is found useful in coughs and flatulence, also as a gentle stimulant in indigestion and stomach complaints.

The dried root is best used in the form of a decoction and the leaves as an infusion. Flavour somewhat like sweet aniseed. Angelica and Sweet Cecily were used in the 17th century to ward off infection at the time of the plague. Possibly the rat fleas did not like the aroma! Perennial, grows best when transplanted, but once established seeds itself freely. Beautiful feathery leaves and very deep-rooted.

Chervil (*Anthriscus cerefolium*)
Annual, grows about 1 ft. high from seed.

Its sweet and aromatic leaves are good for flavouring and salads, very much used in France. Seeds have a very short viability and must be sown the year they are gathered.

Chickweed (*Stellaria media*)
Demulcent, refrigerant.

The fresh leaves are used as a poultice to indolent ulcers with most beneficial results. Is also employed as an application in ophthalmia and as an ointment in skin diseases. In many gardens a pestiferous weed which needs no encouragement!

Chicory, Succory (*Cichorium intybus*)
Tonic, diuretic, laxative.

Culinary: Blanched roots are an excellent mid-winter vegetable or salad. Very pretty blue flower. Grown from seed. Annual.

Witloof. This type of Chicory, which is sometimes called the French Endive, makes a most appetising and delicious salad and can be enjoyed all winter.

Seeds sown May or June produce roots which, when taken up, trimmed and placed in sand in a warm dark place in winter, throw out large tender white sprouts which are used as salad. Grown from seed. Annual.

Medicinal: A decoction of 1 oz. root to 1 pint boiling water, taken freely, has been found effective in jaundice, liver enlargement, gout and rheumatic complaints.

Chives (*Allium schœnoprasum*)
Diuretic and expectorant.

All the members of the Allium family are most excellent and health-giving. Besides being used for culinary purposes often form an ingredient in domestic medicine, e.g. roasted onion as a poultice for suppurating tumours. The juice made into a syrup is excellent as a cough medicine. Chives are small onions which grow in clumps, and the grass is cut and used in salads. The plants die down every winter (unlike the Welsh Onion), a similar plant, which continues all through the year). Chives are a very welcome and nutritious element in a salad. Grown from seed and transplanted.

Comfrey (*Symphytum officinale*)
This very important and useful herb is known sometimes as Knitbone and is indeed marvellous as a poultice in cases of diseased and fractured bones.

126

For tubercular and chest diseases boil an ounce of crushed root in a pint of water for a quarter of an hour, add a pint of milk and simmer for another quarter of an hour. Take a wineglassful three or four times a day. The leaves can be infused in the same way and flavouring such as lemon added, as otherwise it is rather insipid.

The root can be treated as a vegetable and boiled; and the young shoots can be blanched and eaten like asparagus.

This dwarf herb with its white flowers is easily grown and should be in every herb garden for immediate use.

Couchgrass (*Agropyrum repens*)
Diuretic, demulcent, aperient.

This plant, the curse of many a farmer and discouraged by every gardener as a persistent weed, has most excellent medicinal qualities. Dogs and cats partake of it freely whenever possible. It is much used by herbalists in cases of urinary and bladder complaints (cystitis, nephritis, etc.) and is also an aid for gout and rheumatism. The infusion made from 1 oz. of the root in 1 pint of boiling water is taken in wineglassful doses several times daily for feverishness, etc. It is not used in cooking.

Dandelion (*Taraxacum officinale*)
Diuretic, tonic and slightly aperient.

One of the most useful of plants, chiefly used in kidney and liver disorders, and is perhaps one of the most generally prescribed remedies. It may be given in any form, but its beneficial action is best obtained when combined with other agents. It can be had in the form of a roasted root as a substitute for coffee, which possesses most beneficial properties in cases of dyspepsia, gout and rheumatism. The leaves are equally health-giving when used in a raw salad together with the flower heads.

127

Dill (*Anethum graveolens*)
              Carminative, stomachic.
Medicinal: In children's complaints such as flatulence, disordered digestion, etc. an excellent remedy given usually in the form of Dill Water, obtainable at any chemists.
Culinary: The raw foliage in salads.

Fennel (*Fœniculum dulce*)
              Stimulative, carminative, stomachic.
Medicinal: Generally added to other medicines for flavouring, and used as a carminative.
Culinary: The leaves are used for flavouring fish sauces and a small amount can be added to salads.
Can be found growing wild in many hedgerows. In the Italian variety known as *finocchio* the leaf stalks " bulb " at the base and should be earthed up when they begin to swell. In hot climates they should reach the size of a hen's egg and are delicious stewed in stock. Grown from seed.

Feverfew (*Chrysanthemum Parthenium*)
              Aperient, carminative, febrifugal.
Medicinal: Largely used to promote the menses, expel worms and in hysterical conditions. Infusion of 1 oz. to 1 pint of boiling water, taken frequently. The taste is bitter and nauseous, resembling that of tansy.

Garlic (*Allium sativum*)
The " Miracle Herb." Diaphoretic, diuretic and expectorant. One of the most valuable plants in nature. Garlic juice is made into a syrup with honey and given with advantage in coughs, colds and asthma. It also acts as a worm expellant. Oil of Garlic can be obtained in capsules, and also in tablet form, which latter obviates the very pungent smell.

Very much used in cooking on the Continent, especially in Italy, but not nearly enough in Britain. The flavour is akin to onions, but very much stronger.

Every herb garden should have a row of garlic. Easily grown from cloves planted in early spring and harvested in autumn.

Good King Henry (*Chenopodium Bonus Henricus*)

This herb is the richest in iron of any in the garden. It is mainly called the Lincolnshire Spinach as it is still grown there both in gardens and in the wild state. It is called after Henry IV of France. It is one of the Goosefoots. There is a poisonous variety of Goosefoot called *Malus Henricus* (Bad Henry). It is a most excellent blood cleanser and can be eaten cooked like spinach in any quantity. Grows freely from seed and transplanted. Perennial, and increases rapidly, the roots layering profusely. A most valuable herb to cultivate.

Ground Ivy (*Glechoma hederacea*)

Astringent, diuretic, tonic.

Medicinal: Useful in kidney diseases and for indigestion. Also used as an anti-scorbutic. Combined with camomile flowers it makes an excellent poultice for abscesses, gatherings and tumors. The infusion of 1 oz. in 1 pint of boiling water is taken in doses of 1 wineglassful. The taste is bitter and acrid. Grows in profusion in any garden.

Horehound (*Marrubium vulgare*)

Bitter tonic, expectorant, diuretic.

Medicinal: This is perhaps the most popular of herbal pectoral remedies. It is exceedingly valuable in coughs, colds and pulmonary affections. An infusion of 1 oz. to 1 pint of boiling water is taken frequently and is better if well sweetened with honey. The taste is bitter and it is aromatic. Perennial, grown from seed and transplanted.

Hyssop (*Hyssopus officinalis*)
Stimulant, carminative, pectoral.

Also an agreeable remedy in cases of coughs, colds and lung complaints. Generally compounded with other remedies. Infusion of 1 oz. herb leaves to 1 pint boiling water, taken frequently. Perennial grown from seed and transplanted.

Lovage (*Levisticum officinale*)
Diuretic, carminative.

Medicinal: Used in febrile affections and in stomach disorders, also for dysmenorrhoea. The medicine is obtained in a fluid extracted from the rootstock, of which the dose is 5-30 minims.

Culinary: The leaves have a flavor of celery and parsley, and impart a very pleasing taste to soups. The root, which has a similar flavor, is about the size of a parsnip.

Grown from seed and transplanted. Perennial, up to 6 ft. Increases rapidly underground.

Marjoram, Sweet (*Origanum Majorana*)
Tonic, emmenagogic, stimulant.

Hardly ever used in medicine.

Much used in cooking as seasoning. The leaves are added to raw salads and impart a most agreeable aromatic flavor. A volatile oil is made from this plant which is an excellent external application for sprains and bruises.

Annual, grows easily from seed.

Marjoram, Pot (*Origanum vulgare*)
Emmenagogic, stimulant.

The whole herb is medicinal and contains a volatile oil which is separated by distillation. Perspiration may be produced by a warm infusion, which is also taken to promote the menstrual flow when suppressed by cold. The oil is stimulant and often used as a liniment.

Culinary: Very good for flavoring, especially with omelettes. Cut before the flowers open, and dry. Can also be used in little bags to scent linen.

Perennial. Grown easily from seed and transplanted.

Meadowsweet (*Spiræa Ulmaria*)
Aromatic, astringent, diuretic.

Medicinal: Has a pleasant taste, and is incorporated in many herb beers. A good remedy for dropsy and in children's diarrhea, for which it may be deemed a specific. 1 oz. to 1 pint water, taken in wineglassful doses.

Found growing wild in damp meadows.

Melilot (*Melilotus officinalis*)
Aromatic, carminative, emollient.

Relieves flatulence and is taken internally for this purpose. Externally it is applied as a fomentation or poultice for pains and aches. Grown easily from seed.

Mint [Peppermint] (*Mentha piperita*)
Stimulant, stomachic, carminative.

Used for allaying nausea, flatulence, sickness, vomiting, and as an infants' cordial. Generally combined with other medicines when its stomachic effects are required. The infusion of 1 oz. to 1 pint of boiling water is taken frequently in wineglassful doses. It is better sweetened with

honey, and is a sure cure for the onset of a cold, taken hot
before retiring.

Mint [Spearmint] (*Mentha viridis*)

Stimulant, carminative, antispasmodic.
This herb is added to many compounds on account of its
carminative properties and its pleasant taste. The infusion of 1 oz. to 1 pint of boiling water is taken in wineglassful doses as required. For infantile troubles generally,
the infusion sweetened with honey is an excellent remedy.
Grown very easily from transplanted roots and spreads
rapidly.

Nettles (*Urtica urens* and *dioica*)

Diuretic, astringent.
Nettle tea and nettle soup are most excellent, and this is
just the ordinary stinging nettle of the hedgerows that can
be gathered from early spring all the summer. This weed
is high in vitamins A and C. Highly alkaline, a magnificent
spring tonic, it dissolves uric crystals and is therefore the
best medicine for sciatica and rheumatism. Take 2 oz.
nettle juice with 4 oz. carrot juice three times daily, keep
this up all summer and it will give sure relief from urinary
troubles. To make an infusion: 1 oz. of nettle tops and/or
seed to a pint of boiling water. Dose: a wineglassful, taken
frequently.

Parsley (*Carum petroselinum*)

Aperient, diuretic, emmenagogic.
Medicinal: Chiefly used on account of its diuretic qualities.
In cases of gravel, stone, congestion of kidneys and in
dropsy it will be found of great service. The seeds
contain apiol which is considered a safe and efficient
emmenagogue, and is used in amenorrhea and dys-
menorrhea. It can be obtained in capsules.

Culinary: The use of parsley in the kitchen is very well known. It gives a flavor to almost any dish and is especially useful in raw salads.

Parsley can be grown in any garden from seed.

Parsley Piert (*Alchemilla arvensis*)
Demulcent, diuretic.

Used in all cases of gravel, kidney and bladder complaints. It acts directly on the parts affected and will be found exceedingly valuable even in seemingly incurable cases. Several London doctors prescribe this remedy regularly. It is bought as a fluid extract obtainable from chemists. It is not grown in Britain.

Rosemary (*Rosmarinus officinalis*)
Tonic, astringent, diaphoretic.

An excellent stomachic and nervine. Cures many cases of headache. Used externally, an infusion combined with borax makes a good hair wash and will prevent premature baldness. Grown easily from either seed or transplanted roots in any garden in Britain.

Rue (*Ruta graveolens*)
Stimulant, antispasmodic, emmenagogic, digestive.

It is chiefly used in suppression of the menses, but should not be taken in large doses as it is liable to produce inflammations and nerve derangements. For hysteria, amenorrhoea, etc. it will be found valuable. The infusion of 1 oz. to 1 pint water is taken in cupful doses. A few leaves nibbled will ease indigestion. Preparations of the powdered herb and fluid extract are available commercially.

Rue is the only armigerous herb, and figures in the Arms of Scotland.

Sage (*Salvia officinalis*)

Astringent, stimulant, nervine.

Excellent for liver complaints. Sage and honey was a remedy of the olden days for consumption. A decoction of sage is recommended for rheumatism. Sage tea: 1 oz. to 1 pint of boiling water promotes perspiration; laced with lemon and honey it will frequently stave off a cold.

Grown easily in any garden from seed or transplanted roots. Perennial.

Savory [Summer] (*Satureia hortensis*)

Aromatic, carminative.

Chiefly used as a culinary herb. Flavor somewhat like marjoram. Very good served with baked beans. Used for flavorings and stuffings. Annual grown from seed sown in the spring. 1 ft.

Savory [Winter] (*Satureia montana*)

The flavour of this evergreen herb is a little like thyme. It can be used for culinary purposes in the same manner as the summer variety.

Easily grown from seed or transplanted roots in any garden. Does best in poor, well-drained soil. Perennial, 1½ ft.

French Sorrel

The leaves can be chopped up in salads and have a pleasant acid taste. They can also be boiled like spinach, and make a very good sauce to go with duck instead of apple sauce. Grows very easily anywhere from seed or transplanted roots. Perennial, 3 ft.

Tansy (*Tanacetum vulgare*)

Anthelmintic, tonic, emmenagogic.

Largely used for expelling worms in children. Also

valuable in female disorders such as hysteria, nausea, etc. The usual infusion of 1 oz. leaves to 1 pint boiling water should be taken in teacupful doses. The leaves are also useful for seasoning.

Tarragon
Used for flavoring especially in fish sauces and vinegars. Transplanted roots only, no seed. Seed of Russian variety available but is not to be compared to the real French tarragon.

Thyme (*Thymus vulgare*)
Tonic, antiseptic, antispasmodic.
Generally taken in combination with other remedies. The variety known as Lemon thyme (*var. citriodorus*) is much more used for cooking, having all the properties and in addition a very pleasing citrus flavour.

Wormwood (*Artimesia absinthium*)
Tonic, stomachic, febrifugal, anthelmintic.
The most bitter herb in the garden. A good remedy for enfeebled digestion and a great vermifuge. The usual decoction of 1 oz. to 1 pint boiling water should be taken at intervals. This is a main ingredient of absinthe.

I would emphasise again that these are just a few of the more common herbs, the majority of which can be grown in any garden. Dried herbs are available at any health foods store, but there is nothing to compare with the herb freshly gathered.

With few exceptions, I have grown quantities of all these herbs for many years, and I commend a herb garden to my readers for both health and happiness.

CHAPTER 17

Food Reform Recipes

For those who are contemplating turning to food reform and may not be familiar with the cooking and régime generally, I am giving in the following pages a small selection of some vegetarian recipes which I have found excellent. At the end of the book I list a number of suitable books on the subject by authors who can be relied upon entirely.

The standby of every cook is the stock pot. No household need be without vegetable stock for soups if a heavy casserole is used for the cooking. When cooking cabbage, boil it in the stockpot and add onions and apple, with enough water to prevent burning. Leave the residue in the pot for soup, adding leeks and any vegetables you may have. Leave also in the pot any soup you do not require and cook next day's vegetables in it with a little water added. Lentils, split peas, barley, dried mushroom powder (see recipe, p. 105) all help to thicken the soup and add nourishment.

Here is another recipe for stock. Take 1 lb. of haricot beans, pick and wash well and soak for 12 hours (overnight) in cold water. Put them in the saucepan with the water in which they were soaked, add a few of the coarser stalks of celery, 1 or 2 chopped onions, a blade of mace and some white peppercorns. Bring to the boil and cook gently for at least 2 hours. Then strain and use as required.

A FEW VEGETARIAN SOUPS

Rich Gravy Soup

If this is well made it is as good as anything cooked by a professional chef.

To 3 pints of haricot stock add 1 onion and 1 carrot (fried with butter until brown), 1 stick of celery, 2 turnips and 6 peppercorns and thicken with cornflour. Boil all together for 1 hour, strain and return to saucepan and add 3 teaspoonfuls of yeast extract (Marmite or Yeastrel or similar). Warm it up, but not to boiling point. Serve with fried bread dice.

Leek Soup

This excellent recipe comes from Flanders and is very easy and cheap to make. Chop up a handful of sorrel, two of chervil, half a dozen leeks and a couple of lettuces. Cook them all in one of the above stocks with a little butter and a pinch of basil, which can be bought easily if not grown in the herb garden. Add half a dozen potatoes peeled and cut in quarters. Let all this cook very slowly for 4 or 5 hours, then mash up the potatoes in the soup and serve.

Then of course there is the famous *Potage Parmentier* of which there are several versions. I think the following method is as good as any. Peel 1 lb. of potatoes and cut them in quarters. Cut the white part of three leeks into thin slices and fry them in a little butter until they are soft but not browned. To them add the potatoes and 1½ pints of hot water. Season with salt and put on the lid, bring to the boil and boil quickly for 20 minutes or so. When the potatoes are soft pass them through a wire sieve, rinse the saucepan, put the purée back into it, bring just to the boil and simmer very gently for 5 minutes. Correct the seasoning, adding pepper, take the pan off the fire, stir in two egg yolks beaten up with a little milk, cream or yogurt and add at the last a small piece of butter. Serve very hot with croûtons of fried bread.

Potage Solferino

Cut up an onion and the white part of three leeks into thin slices and let them stew without browning in an ounce or so of butter. Add 3 pints of vegetable stock and bring to the boil. Add now ¾ lb. of tomatoes and ½ lb. potatoes cut in slices, and a clove of garlic. Cover and simmer for half an hour or until the potatoes are cooked. Rub through a fine sieve, heat up again and serve garnished with French beans. An addition of a small quantity of chopped herbs, chervil, marjoram and a touch of cayenne in the seasoning improves the flavour.

Vermicelli Soup

This is a South American recipe. The ingredients are:

> 2 oz. vermicelli. 3 oz. vegetable fat or butter. 1 lb. tomatoes peeled and sliced. 1 large onion, minced. 1½ tablespoonfuls parsley, chopped. 2 pints vegetable stock. 1½ oz. grated cheese. A pinch cayenne pepper. A pinch of saffron.

Heat the butter in a stewpan, fry the onions and parsley for 3 minutes, add vermicelli and fry for 2 minutes until light brown, but be careful not to burn it. Add the tomatoes and saffron and cook gently for 5 minutes. Pour on the stock, bring to the boil and simmer until the vermicelli is tender. Add the seasonings, sprinkle with cheese, and serve.

Haricot Bean Soup

An Italian recipe. The ingredients are:

1 lb. haricot beans. ½ red cabbage. 2 or 3 onions. 2 leeks. 1 head of celery. A clove garlic (crushed). A sprig of thyme. Seasoning. 4 tablespoonfuls olive oil. 2 table-spoonfuls of tomato purée. 3 pints of stock.

Soak the haricot beans overnight, put them in a casserole with the olive oil, tomato purée and the chopped vegetables, season with salt, pepper and herbs. Add the stock and simmer slowly for at least 2 hours.

CHAPTER 18

Homeopathy

I am frequently asked if I believe in homeopathy, and I certainly do. The principles are right and the treatment is in any case entirely harmless. Homeopathy was founded over a hundred years ago by a renowned physician, Dr. Hahnemann, on the supposition that " Like cures like " (*Similia similibus curantur*). All the medicines used are made from herbs, vegetables and minerals and are therefore entirely natural medicines, as distinct from drugs manufactured from chemicals, and cannot possibly do any harm to the tissues, nor form any dangerous habits.

The theory and practice of homeopathy is based on the fact that the human body is composed of an enormous number of tiny living cells, each one made up of an infinitesimal but perfectly balanced quantity of three classes of materials—water, organic substances and inorganic substances. Water and organic matter, such as sugar, albuminous and fatty substances make up the greater part of the body. The inorganic (mineral) elements, however, although present in very much smaller quantities, are really vital elements—the active workers which utilize the inactive organic substances in building the millions of cells of which the body is composed. All living organisms are made up of countless living cells, each of which is a small chemical factory in itself. Minute traces of many chemical salts are contained in, and are necessary to, these cells. The supply of these chemicals, or trace elements as they are known, must be maintained if the living organism, be it man, animal or plant, is to be kept in health. These trace elements are indeed just that, traces and no more.

The principle of homeopathy is easy to understand by taking a bee sting as an example. It is well known that the irritation is caused by a minute injection of formic acid through the sting. (Incidentally this formic acid is also present in minute quantities in the honey, and is thought to be a cure for rheumatism). To counteract the irritation and effects of the sting, homeopathy takes a drop of the bee venom and breaks the molecules into an enormous number of atoms and administers a dilution of this, which nullifies the sting.

By and large, this is the general principle. Like cures like. And note that the homeopathic chemist, who has to be a very skilled pharmacist, uses only medicines that have first been " organised " by the vegetable kingdom. The human body can absorb only those things which have first been made by the vegetable kingdom, and this Rule of Medicines, in accordance with Natural Law, is the Law of Homeopathy.

But there is something more. The theory and practice of this most excellent method of treating disease is that it is not sufficient to treat the trouble on the surface, but that it is necessary to find the basic *cause* of the trouble, and a practising homeopathic consultant may have to spend a considerable time at a first interview to fill in the background and find out the reason for the sickness. Only when this has been established can he prescribe for a permanent cure. And all his efforts are devoted to aiding Nature.

I have referred in this book to the great Hippocrates, the Father of Medicine, and his contention was that " Nature cures—not the physician." Modern medicine loses sight of the fact that it is the whole man that is sick, not just a part or a particular organ. Serious consequences are often the result when surgical intervention is used in an attempt to cure disease by removing an affected part or tumor without first attacking it through its symptoms in the first case. No organ can live independently of any other organ, no more than it can become diseased by itself, for the reason that it depends on every other organ for some part of its life.

All the correct homeopathic remedy is supposed to do is to correct the deranged action of the vital force, after which this vital force acts naturally in conformity with the laws of nature. Often a changed mentality gives the key to the remedy. Every physical or mental derangement is first a disordered vitality, just as every cure is restored vitality. Medicine to be successful must go farther than just mechanism.

Homeopathy can cure most diseases quickly and without any danger of after-effects.

CHAPTER 19

Poison in the Kitchen

I cannot conclude this book without drawing attention to two dangers. The first concerns the aluminium cooking utensils so frequently used in kitchens these days.

In one of his excellent books on special subjects, Mr. J. I. Rodale remarks: " There is not the slightest doubt in my mind that aluminium utensils for cooking are dangerous to human health, and one should ban them from the kitchen."

Mr. Rodale goes on to give some most impressive facts and figures in support of his contention, and with his permission I shall quote a few here. He found, by experiment on himself, that drinking coffee made in a glass pot did not raise his pulse a single point, but when made in an aluminium pot it raised the pulse, on an average, 7 to 8 points per minute. He quotes an account in the American *Poultry Tribune* for September, 1951. Describing a method of removing tarnish from silver, which is referred to as " an almost effortless way," you must start with an *aluminium* container, says the item. (The word " aluminium " is in italics, showing that no other metal will do the job.) Then you fill it with water and put in enough table salt to make an extra heavy solution—to such an extent that some of the salt stands in the bottom of the container. You then place the silverware to be cleaned in this solution and heat it up until it boils for three minutes. Then your silver will be shining bright. . . . There is apparently something in aluminium, then, which in combination with something that is in salt is powerful enough to remove tarnish from silver. This is the one time when it is helpful to have an aluminium pan in the kitchen.

Now it can be realized what cooking anything containing baking soda in aluminium will do. Add a pinch of soda to the water cooking peas and it turns them a brighter green. There must be enough aluminium etched off by the baking soda to enter into a chemical action with the peas to cause such a radical change of colour. Has anyone ever turned peas a brighter green in stainless steel?

Some aluminium-ware manufacturers advise the use of oxalic acid crystals as a cleaning solution. This is a dangerously corrosive poison, which incidentally is contained in considerable amounts in spinach and rhubarb. These vegetables are not harmful if eaten in moderation, but should be avoided by persons with kidney disease, and should *never* be cooked in aluminium. Sauerkraut is another vegetable that should never touch aluminium. It will produce aluminium chloride, especially if allowed to stand.

Dr. Le Hunte Cooper, R.A.M.C., records that he found that some of the aluminium taken in is cumulative in the human system. A famous London consultant also states that the defenders of alumium stand on the ground that the amount of aluminium which reaches the system is harmless. But the fact is that a chemical substance may do more harm in the body by the dissemination of its activity, which cannot be detected, than by its mass.

The best material for cooking is oven-proof glassware; then comes the *best* enamel ware; third, stainless steel. Porcelain is perfect for food storage.

The second danger is the slow poison called salt. A long time ago Professor Jacques Loeb stated that sodium chloride is toxic to protoplasm. Ordinary common salt is practically pure sodium chloride and, as such, is poisonous to the tissues in the human body. To make this product non-toxic it is necessary to add a small percentage of potassium chloride to the common salt.

An average consumption of salt can be put at about 300 grains per day. Without the balancing potassium chloride the body will not be able to utilise very much of this—say about 15 grains—leaving over 280 grains to be disposed of by the body and, if the kidneys and sweat glands do not succeed in carrying off the excess, harmful deposition gradually occurs which does immense harm to the tissues. It is the considered opinion of those scientists who have made a study of the subject that taking quantities of salt which is not balanced by potassium and other physiological salts is helping to cause such troubles as catarrh, bronchial affections, kidney and heart disorders and hardening of the arteries, among other diseases. In fact, some doctors have described common salt (sodium chloride) as the most active cancer cause amongst inorganic agents. Potassium salts have the opposite effect and there are records of treatment of inoperable cases of cancer being treated with potassium salts with great success. Dr. Henry Gilbert, who studied the subject very deeply, said that when the balance between sodium and potassium is upset by eating common salt, actual displacement of cellular potassium does occur, and sodium, which in normal proportions is a natural constituent of the body, then acts as a cytoplasmic toxin, and that it cannot be eliminated except by potassium salts that can act upon the cell walls in a particular way.

Dr. Gilbert also made some very careful calculations as to the amounts of potassium salts that must be combined with sodium chloride to make it non-toxic, and as a result his non-toxic salt under the name of *The Salt of Life* is now available and is stocked by health food stores throughout the country.

Index

147

INDEX

Books on Health and Nutrition

VITAMIN E
Your Key to a Healthy Heart
Herbert Bailey

WHY IS VITAMIN E therapy for mankind's foremost killing disease still controversial in the United States? This is one of the questions asked and answered in this slashing, fully-documented book. It tells how the efficacy of vitamin E in the treatment of cardiovascular disease was discovered by Dr. Evan Shute of Canada, and of the remarkable cures effected by him and his brother, also a doctor . . . how the author himself suffered a severe heart attack and how in a short time he was restored to normal active life by massive doses of the vitamin . . . how a barrier against vitamin E has been erected in this country by the medical traditionalists of the American Medical Association at the same time that it is being widely used with spectacular results in such medically-advanced countries as England, Germany, France, Italy, and Russia . . . how continuing study indicates that vitamin E may be an effective preventive for diabetes, sterility, arthritis and a variety of other diseases. "Literally worth its weight in gold."
—The Pittsburgh Courier   **$1.65**

GET WELL NATURALLY
Linda Clark

LINDA CLARK believes that relieving human suffering and obtaining optimum health should be mankind's major goal. She insists that it does not matter whether a remedy is orthodox or unorthodox, currently praised or currently scorned in medical circles—as long as it works for you. Miss Clark, who is also the author of **Stay Young Longer,** makes a plea for the natural methods of treating disease—methods which do not rely on either drugs or surgery. Drawing not only from well-known sources but also from folklore and from the more revolutionary modern theories, she presents a wealth of information about diseases ranging from alcoholism to ulcers. Here are frank discussions of such controversial modes of treatment as herbal medicine, auto-therapy, homeopathy, and human electronics, plus some startling facts and theories about nutrition and about the natural ways of treating twenty-two of the most serious illnesses that plague modern man.   **$1.65**

FOOD FACTS AND FALLACIES
Carlton Fredericks and Herbert Bailey

A noted nutritionist and veteran medical reporter present medical evidence based on modern research to prove that a good diet can lessen your effects of coming down with one of today's common health problems, such as heart disease, arthritis, mental illness, and many others. This book gives the unadulterated facts about fad diets, and it presents some startling information about proper diet and the prevention and treatment of alcoholism. To help you be sure that you are getting the balanced meals you need, the authors have included eleven rules for menu selection; tips on buying meats, cereals, and breads; lists of common sources of vitamins, carbohydrates, and fats; and an appendix of suggested menus.   **$1.75**

LOW BLOOD SUGAR AND YOUR HEALTH
Eat Your Way Out of Fatigue
Clement G. Martin, M.D.

In this revolutionary new book, Dr. Martin tells exactly how to determine if hypoglycemia is the cause of fatigue problems, and if so, he outlines a diet that can make anyone feel better after the first week. It's not a starvation diet, not a fad diet. But it is unusual. The Doctor instructs the reader to eat eight times a day rather than three. And for those who don't suffer from hypoglycemia, it is still probable that the cause of the fatigue or mental distress is nutrition. These people will find Dr. Martin's delicious, eight-times-a-day diet pouring new energy into their bodies.

This is not a book of "miracle cures." It is a book about common sense attitudes toward nutrition and exercise—proof positive that a sensible, well-balanced diet is the **real** key to good health.   **$1.65**

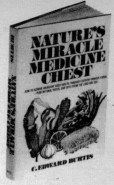

NATURE'S MIRACLE MEDICINE CHEST

C. Edward Burtis

How to achieve abundant good health through everyday wonder foods—pure natural foods, our gifts from the land and sea. Mr. Burtis covers many of the wonder foods found in nature's miracle medicine chest and explains how to use them for better health—the fantastic papaya melon, digestive disorders and the lime, slipped discs and vitamin C, cabbage juice and ulcers, yogurt and digestive health, calcium and the heart, bone meal and loose teeth, garlic and diarrhea, the bactericidal qualities of honey, the remarkable powers of royal jelly, kelp for the common cold, cod liver oil and arthritis, vitamin E and the heart, brewer's yeast as a protective agent, sesame seeds as a tranquilizer.

Clothbound, $5.95

COMMON AND UNCOMMON USES OF HERBS FOR HEALTHFUL LIVING

Richard Lucas

A fascinating account of the herbal remedies used through the ages. Plant medicine has been used for thousands of years and modern science is now re-evaluating many old-time herbal medicines. Described here are the herbal folk remedies that have been used for centuries by the American Indians, the gypsies, the ancient herbalists, the countryfolk, and the old-time country doctor. The background, history and uses of such healing herbs as dandelion, elder, nettle, sage, kelp, onion, parsley, sassafras, rosemary, camomile, corn silk, celery as cures for rash, hives, urinary disorders, ulcers, gout, and nervous disorders are described. **$1.65**

THE LOW-FAT WAY TO HEALTH AND LONGER LIFE

Lester Morrison, M.D.

The famous best-seller that has helped millions gain robust health and increased life span through simple changes in diet, the use of nutritional supplements and weight control. With menus, recipes, life-giving diets, and programs endorsed by distinguished medical authorities. **$1.65**

CARLSON WADE'S HEALTH FOOD RECIPES FOR GOURMET COOKING   Carlson Wade

Hundreds of recipes for preparing natural health foods—gourmet style—for healthful eating pleasure. The secret of youthful energy and vitality is in the magical powers of vitamins, minerals, enzymes, protein, and other life-giving elements found in **natural foods.** In this new book, noted nutrition expert Carlson Wade shows you how you can make delicious meals prepared with pure, natural foods; seeds, nuts, berries, whole grains, honey, fruits, fish and more. **$1.65**

INTERNATIONAL VEGETARIAN COOKERY

Sonya Richmond

This book proves that vegetarian cookery, far from being dull and difficult to prepare, can open up completely new and delightful vistas of haute cuisine. Miss Richmond, who has traveled throughout the world, has arranged the book alphabetically according to countries, starting with Austria and going through to the United States. She gives recipes for each country's most characteristic vegetarian dishes and lists that country's outstanding cheeses.

Clothbound: $3.75
Paperbound: $1.95

HOW TO BE HEALTHY WITH NATURAL FOODS
Edward G. Marsh

Do you feel sluggish, tired, old beyond your years? Do you get frequent colds, lack pep and energy, feel overweight and stuffed? Chances are that you are not eating the right foods. The average American's diet today consists of innutritious processed foods, fats and starches, insufficient vitamins and minerals—a diet that contains little or nothing of value and, usually, much that is downright harmful. **HOW TO BE HEALTHY WITH NATURAL FOODS** shows that it is possible to maintain optimum health and eliminate colds and other chronic ailments by using only wholesome, natural foods and by eliminating from your diet foods that are harmful or that contain nothing of value to your body. In this concise, practical book on nutrition, the author presents simple, tried and tested rules for the selection of healthful and tasty foods, including suggestions for specific diets to build and maintain vitality, protect against senility, and promote vigorous health and long life. **$1.50**

THE SOYBEAN COOKBOOK
Mildred Lager & Dorothea Van Gundy Jones

Soybeans . . . almost as old as civilization . . . are today the newest and most exciting phenomenon in the nutrition field. This book fills the urgent need for a comprehensive cookbook dealing with this nutritious and versatile food. Included here are over 350 recipes for delicious ways to use soybeans in dishes ranging from salads to souffles to desserts. Each recipe has many zestful variations, and the book offers suggestions for using the beans in all their many forms, including soy flour, dried soybeans, cooked green soybeans, soy oil, and soy sprouts. Also included is a discussion of the soybean's nutritional value and a brief history of its uses.

Clothbound: $4.50
Paperbound: $1.45

HEALTH FOODS AND HERBS
Kathleen Hunter

The advantages of eating only natural foods are discussed in this comprehensive guide to healthful living. Included are many easy-to-prepare recipes made with mushrooms, yogurt, cheese, fresh vegetables, seaweed, nuts, honey, and other untreated foods plus extensive information on using herbs—both for medicinal and culinary purposes. Miss Hunter also discusses the important vitamin groups, chemical fertilizers, and the safest types of cooking utensils.

Clothbound: $4.50
Paperbound: $1.50